D0584616

Wendy Heyn has done a fantastic job of telling these moms' very personal and challenging stories, while at the same time showing the support and strength which God alone could give them through his Word. I had several of my staff members read through Wendy's book. They are all excited about it. One of them, herself a mother of a child with special needs, wrote at the end of her copy: "A wonderful use of the stories of Mary. This book is a gem! . . . The variety of situations covers so many parents." I agree wholeheartedly.

Pastor Joel Gaertner
National Director, Jesus Cares Ministries

Wendy Heyn and eight other mothers are remarkably candid and authentic in sharing their experiences of parenting children with special needs in *Show Me Your Mighty Hand*. Their stories are a source of great encouragement and support to Christian families seeking to make sense of God's purposes through their experience of disability.

Stephen Grcevich, MD
Clinical Associate Professor of Psychiatry,
Northeast Ohio Medical University
President and Founder, Key Ministry

In the seemingly least likely passage of God's Word, Wendy Heyn lovingly weaves the realities of parenting a child with a serious diagnosis with the emotions of our Savior's mother. With profound insight, she exposes God's matchless character through individual stories of families' difficulties on the journey. Readers are sure to enjoy a fresh encounter with their Maker and boundless hope in this unique book for mothers raising children with special needs.

Barb Dittrich
Executive Director, Snappin Ministries

So many of us are parenting in the sea of unexpected. . . . Unexpected journeys with our kiddos that we never anticipated and we do not know how to swim through or even wade in. . . . And then there is Jesus. And then there is HOPE. Wendy weaves her HOPE-filled story beautifully and honestly with Jesus. And then she offers her readers the HOPE of knowing they are not alone. They are standing with a rag-tag army of families parenting unexpected and uncharted territory, and Jesus walks with each of them and each of us. For the parent of a child with special needs, this is a must-read.

Jackie Hooks
Founder, Pruning Hooks Ministries

Woven through the book are God's comforting answers. . . . Such a powerful testament to God's grace and mercy.

Anna Geiger
www.themeasuredmom.com

The mothers in these stories hold nothing back. Their honest and raw emotions will meet your honest and raw emotions, and their scars will resonate with your own. Their honesty doesn't leave us without answers, though. Story after story reminds us that while God doesn't always answer our prayers the way we hoped he would, he doesn't abandon us either.

Amber Albee Swenson
www.holyhenhouse.com

Show Me Your Mighty Hand

Peace From God's Word for Special-Needs Moms

Wendy Heyn

NORTHWESTERN PUBLISHING HOUSE
Milwaukee, Wisconsin

Cover illustrations: Debbie Peterson, Shutterstock
Art Director: Karen Knutson
Designer: Sarah Messner

All Scripture quotations, unless otherwise indicated, are taken from the Holy Bible, New International Version®, NIV®. Copyright © 1973, 1978, 1984, 2011 by Biblica, Inc.™ Used by permission of Zondervan. All rights reserved worldwide. www.zondervan.com.

The "NIV" and "New International Version" are trademarks registered in the United States Patent and Trademark Office by Biblica, Inc.™

Hymn references marked CWS are taken from *Christian Worship: Supplement* © 2008 by Northwestern Publishing House.

Northwestern Publishing House
1250 N. 113th St., Milwaukee, WI 53226-3284
www.nph.net
© 2016 Northwestern Publishing House
Published 2016
Printed in the United States of America
ISBN 978-0-8100-2794-7
ISBN 978-0-8100-2795-4 (e-book)

CONTENTS

♥ ♥ ♥

FOREWORD

Claps and cheers for Wendy Heyn.

Everybody likes to hear the stories of successful, good-looking, smart kids. Christmas family brag letters don't usually talk about school dropouts, endless doctor and hospital visits, child-sized wheelchairs, or any of the many kinds of brokenness that you will find in families everywhere. And I mean everywhere. Just in my own close family, for example, confused and nervous parents have had to deal with Williams syndrome, autism, hydrocephaly, childhood cancer, and a stillbirth, not to mention numerous miscarriages. Special-needs children mess with the tidy career plans of their parents, and their unique demands can put a heavy strain on marriages. These demands can be crushing for a single parent to manage.

Our broken world, still reeling under the invasion of death, sickness, and myriad disabilities, produces broken children too. They are not God's punishments on bad parents. They are precious human beings with special needs that God entrusts to us, hoping not only to protect and help them but also to change us and make us more useful for his agenda. We are all broken, and special-needs children do a lot of ministry in God's unique bottom-up way.

If you are the parent of a special-needs child, I hope you find the strength God gives through huddling with your fellow special-needs parents, through the sweet fellowship of your congregation, through serving your stressed spouse even when you think you are the one who needs extra spousal attention, and now with this book through Wendy Heyn's stories and wisdom. May you come to accept the holy mission of tending to the "least of these brothers and sisters" of Jesus (Matthew 25:40). The more you adopt the posture of a servant, the more God will lift you up.

You are his all-stars. Thank you for all you do.

Pastor Mark Jeske

♥ ♥ ♥

CHAPTER 1

Trying to Praise God

WENDY'S STORY

Motherhood has been quite a surprise for me—not the having a baby part, but the actual life after the babies part.

Growing up, I was always watching my own mom. I have spent my life surrounded by moms—the moms of friends, classmates, cousins, neighbors—and I watched them too. I was a babysitter, a nanny, and a camp counselor during my teen and young adult years. Later, I spent nearly a decade teaching early elementary school. In a way, I have spent my whole life studying for the role of motherhood. With all of my exposure to mothers and practice at caring for children, I expected that motherhood would hold very few surprises and that I would be quite good at being a mother.

Imagine my surprise, then, these past years, when nearly every day of motherhood has stretched me in so many ways. I never knew that as a mom, the heat of daily expectations would magnify so many of my weaknesses. I never realized that motherhood would force me to my knees every single day, asking God to work somehow through my mistakes.

Motherhood is packed full of unexpected happenings. It is messy. It doesn't matter how I plan, pray, and try to keep order—my family life becomes messy. That messiness always shatters my expectations and desire for an orderly home and a calm family. Unexpected and messy things are a challenge for me. Learning to see God's mighty hand in the midst of the unexpected and messy has been difficult for me in my life as a mom.

In my home I often find things in unexpected places. I find science experiments under beds and on windowsills. I find candy melted into the cracks in my car and fruit smashed within small jeans pockets. My youngest enjoys pretending that she is packing bags to go places: many small objects go missing only to turn up later packed into small bags and purses. I find dolls put away in containers that are neatly labeled "cars," socks in the drawer neatly labeled "pants," stray puzzle pieces and game cards littering the bottoms of backpacks. Although I spend a lot of time organizing and cleaning our home, I just cannot keep up with our little disorganizers.

The same is true for the time in my days. I wake up with a plan. Get the older kids fed and on their buses: a crazy race of urging and prodding to get them where they need to be. Once the big kids are off to school, it's time for all the things I have planned for my youngest and me to accomplish before they get back home. But then the unexpected messes up my plans: phone calls from the doctor, notes from the teachers, babysitters cancelling, owies needing tending, needs for a potty on that quick grocery run, potty accidents, etc. And those are just the smaller surprises.

───── ❤ ❤ ❤ ─────

Sometimes the reality of Liam's syndrome feels unexpected, even though we have been living with it for eight years.

There are big unexpected things too: lost jobs, unexpected bills, unexpected pregnancies, unexpected illnesses, and many others, life altering and faith altering.

For our family, the biggest unexpected thing has been our second child Liam's developmental delays and the subsequent diagnosis of his MECP2 duplication syndrome. For Liam, MECP2 duplication syndrome means that he is entirely nonverbal, has severe physical disabilities, and has very complex medical issues. Liam's special needs give our already busy and messy days a new variety of unexpectedness.

Sometimes the reality of Liam's syndrome feels unexpected, even though we have been living with it for eight years. There are days when I look around my house and feel shocked by the reality of it. I see Liam's wheelchair. I see our shelves stacked with big-boy-sized diapers. I see the wheelchair ramp into our home. I see my adapted van. I see my sweet son who at eight years old is unable to walk. I remind myself that I have never heard Liam's voice say words. I think about a typical eight-year-old running, reading, playing, singing, and talking. I say to myself, "I have a child who is so very disabled?! Really?" Then of course I know that yes, indeed, it is true! Wow. It feels like somewhere inside of me I just cannot absorb this unexpected news. After eight years of feeding Liam three meals (spoonful by spoonful), giving him five drinks (as I hold and tip the cup), and caring for his personal needs with no help at all from him every single day, this reality still feels surprising. After eight years of learning about and advocating for services for Liam, this reality still feels surprising. After eight years of managing Liam's complex web of health care providers, this reality still feels surprising. After eight years of looking into his precious blue eyes, rejoicing in every milestone met, and loving our precious boy, there are still moments of realization when I have that head-to-toe, body-jarring kind of surprise as I absorb the reality of Liam's disabilities.

I keenly remember my very first of those reality-absorbing moments—when the doctor called and gave us Liam's diagnosis. As I hung up the phone that day, my heart was not at that moment full of praises for my great God or seeing his mighty hand at work. I can remember the table and the tile and the look on the face of the genetic counselor who met with us the following week to explain what MECP2 duplication meant. (Because, really, who has ever heard of MECP2 duplication syndrome?!) When she looked at us with tears in her eyes and explained this syndrome that is (from an earthly point of view) quite bleak, my heart's impulse was not to talk of the greatness and grace of my God. My immediate thoughts were shock and devastation. I thought of Liam never getting married. I thought of Liam never graduating high school. I thought of how Liam's sister would never fight with or chase or tease or play with her brother as a typical sibling would. I felt shame because MECP2 duplication syndrome is maternally inherited. I felt great fear about the future. How could I face years and years of care and diapering and doctoring? I thought of the faces of disabled adults that I had met, and I thought, "NO! Not my beautiful baby!" My next thoughts? No, my friends, they were still not praise thoughts. My next thoughts were reasoning and sifting through information. Would Liam walk? Would Liam talk? Would he have a job someday? Who are the best doctors, therapists, and teachers to help him be as "normal" as possible? I'm sorry to say that it took me a while to get to the praise part.

In the face of MECP2 duplication syndrome, my heart's first impulse has not been to praise God. Even when his mighty hand was nearly impossible to ignore, I often failed to see it. In my wrecked state of mind (it truly was so very wrecked), I knew well that God wants me to praise him and is worthy of my praise no matter what the circumstances. But my first impulse was not to find confidence and comfort in the protection of God's mighty hand. My focus really wasn't on my God. It was on my son and his diagnosis and on my own pain. I am so thankful for a Christian husband, family, friends, and church members who reminded me to turn to God's Word.

I searched the Scriptures for solace, and in them, over and over, God told me, "I am still worthy of your praises." He created the mountains and the valleys. He knit me together in my mother's womb. While I was still a sinner, he loved me enough to send his Son to die in my place. His heavenly home has a place for me. These are big reasons to keep praising God—even in the face of MECP2 duplication syndrome. My God's greatness felt overshadowed by my heartache and Liam's disability. The reality, though, is that God's greatness remained the same. Before Liam's diagnosis, God was the loving God who sent his Son to die for me. After Liam's diagnosis, he was that very same God. My situation had changed, but God's love and presence hadn't. "My mouth will speak in praise of the Lord. Let every creature praise his holy name for ever and ever" (Psalm 145:21). So I praised him.

I praised out of obedience, not from a praise-filled heart. I continued to study God's Word and worship, but with great emptiness and thankless feelings in my heart. Though my heart felt empty and my praises rang hollow, God's hand hadn't lost its might. His Word and Holy Spirit continued their work in my heart. God carried me, sending his people with the hands of Christ to hold me and help so that I could keep going during those first days. These people, the hands and feet of Christ, reminded me that I have joy, in my God, even when earthly circumstances aren't easy or happy, even when I don't *feel* joyful. They kept pointing me to God's Word. That's what I needed them to do. They wouldn't let me forget: my God hadn't changed. He was the same great God that he had been before we heard the words *MECP2 duplication syndrome.* I called to God and begged him to fix my son, and I know it was the Holy Spirit's doing that I was still even on speaking terms with God. But the Spirit didn't stop there. He kept at work in me, using his Word to change how I saw my son. God was carrying me in so many ways! I looked at my little son, and he was the same sweet, happy, beloved boy that he had been the day before we heard he had a "syndrome." He was still a beloved little child of God. As I reflected on God's Word and the promises of the gospel, my heart was changed and my praises became heartfelt. The very words I was using to praise God caused my eyes to turn to my God and helped me see Liam's eternal purpose and God's great love for him.

Eight years later, I still have many times when my praise isn't heartfelt praise, only obedient praise. The days can be difficult, and the hurts are deep. My heart sometimes feels tempted to think that my God isn't praiseworthy because of my difficult circumstances. My head knows that we serve a great God who is absolutely worthy of my praise all the time and that his mighty hand is at work in our lives. My Bible and my Christian support system remind me of the greatness of my God. Whenever I praise my God in obedience, his Holy Spirit has a chance to put those words to work and change my heart again. He works gratitude and awe for my glorious God into my hurting heart.

I would like you to compare my reaction to the news of Liam's diagnosis with the reaction of Mary, Jesus' mother, to some very different, yet still very life-changing, news.

> God sent the angel Gabriel to Nazareth, a town in Galilee, to a virgin pledged to be married to a man named Joseph, a descendant of David. The virgin's name was Mary. The angel went to her and said, "Greetings, you who are highly favored! The Lord is with you."

> Mary was greatly troubled at his words and wondered what kind of greeting this might be. But the angel said to her, "Do not be afraid, Mary; you have found favor with God. You will conceive and give birth to a son, and you are to call him Jesus. He will be great and will be called the Son of the Most High. The Lord God will give him the throne of his father David, and he will reign over Jacob's descendants forever; his kingdom will never end."

> "How will this be," Mary asked the angel, "since I am a virgin?"

> The angel answered, "The Holy Spirit will come on you, and the power of the Most High will overshadow you. So the holy one to be born will be called the Son of God. Even Elizabeth your relative is going to have a child in her old age, and she who was said to be unable to conceive is

in her sixth month. For no word from God will ever fail."

"I am the Lord's servant," Mary answered. "May your word to me be fulfilled." Then the angel left her. (Luke 1:26-38)

Mary was a simple young Jewish girl. She knew the promises of God that one day he would send a Savior. Mary was engaged to be married to a man named Joseph. She was a virgin. During her day and time, an unmarried woman who became pregnant might be stoned to death. So when the angel Gabriel visited Mary and told her that she would become pregnant by the power of the Holy Spirit and that she would become the mother of Jesus, our Savior, surely it meant that her life would be very different than she had ever dreamed of or expected. There were real consequences for Mary to fear. Mary knew that her family, friends, neighbors, and Joseph himself would think that she had slept with some other man. We aren't told in the Bible what Mary's worries or concerns were. How would she have felt as she thought about her new future? What thoughts must she have had? Did she still have any hope for her marriage? Did she fear for her life?

While this news from the angel meant that the world would have eternal salvation, it also meant that Mary would face some very unexpected circumstances. It seems she was able to absorb her new reality so very quickly: her immediate response was "I am the Lord's servant. May your word to me be fulfilled."

Not long after this—maybe only a week later—we get to know the heart of Mary a bit better when we hear her beautiful song of praise.

And Mary said:

"My soul glorifies the Lord
and my spirit rejoices in God my Savior,
for he has been mindful
of the humble state of his servant.
From now on all generations
will call me blessed,
for the Mighty One has done
great things for me—
holy is his name.
His mercy extends to
those who fear him,
from generation to generation.
He has performed mighty
deeds with his arm;
he has scattered those who are
proud in their inmost thoughts.
He has brought down rulers
from their thrones
but has lifted up the humble.
He has filled the hungry
with good things
but has sent the rich away empty.
He has helped his servant Israel,
remembering to be merciful to Abraham
and his descendants forever,
just as he promised our ancestors."
(Luke 1:46-55)

Yes, the kind of unexpected motherhood news Mary got was very different from mine. But I think, even so, you can see quite a contrast between my reactions and Mary's. There have been times when I have looked at Mary and felt unworthy or guilty that my responses are so often not like hers. An attitude that says to God, "I am your servant"? A heart overflowing with praise? Unquestioning trust in God's mighty hand? I have found Mary hard to relate to. I don't think I'm much like her.

Then again, the more I have thought about Mary, read the sections of Scripture that tell about her, and prayed that God would guide me as I studied her, the more I realize I'm missing the point of her story if all I get out of it is feelings of guilt and unworthiness. The point of Mary's story is that God put into her womb his own Son, come to be the Savior of the guilty and unworthy.

❤ ❤ ❤

I'm missing the point of Mary's story if all I get out of it is feelings of guilt and unworthiness.

Jesus loved me enough to die for my sins. He extends grace to me even though he knows my every weakness. He knew my first responses weren't going to be praise, but he loves me anyway. He saved me anyway. *And* he has forgiven my lack of praise. I can look at Mary without guilt or shame and see her as an example I want to try more to live up to. I can pray that the Holy Spirit would continue to work in me so that my heart would be filled with praise in every situation. God promises he will "give the Holy Spirit to those who ask him" (Luke 11:13).

Mary's situation with her son was difficult. However, the challenges of the virgin pregnancy and birth were only the beginning. Childhood would have been full of the unexpected as well. Jesus was fully human, but he wasn't an average boy. He was God. However many moms Mary had watched growing up, she had never seen how to be a good mom when your child is God. Moreover, even at a young age, Jesus' fame reached to other nations and awakened powerful, violent enemies. This was so different than the normal motherhood that Mary would have grown up expecting or hoped for when she became engaged to Joseph. At this point, despite her unexpected news, Mary had her eyes fixed on her God. How well did she keep them fixed there? Over the years, did it get hard for her to keep her focus on God's plan and purpose? Was Mary able to see God's mighty hand at work in her life?

Mary's situations, the words spoken to her, and her words of response resonate in my mind. They move me because I, like Mary, am the mother of a different kind of son. I have lived the unexpected announcement. It wasn't of a Savior, but of a different kind of life and an adjustment to my plans. I am living a life that I never imagined would be mine. I am learning to navigate. I am praying through the difficulties. I am learning to praise through them as well.

My son is very different and so was Mary's. When I hear about Mary, I identify with her. She and I are two moms who have a great God. We have a Savior. We have the promise of heaven. We are two moms who are trying to navigate through an earthly life that we never expected. We are each trying to keep our eyes on our God, even while the devil puts difficulties and hardships in our paths. Mary's example is a profound one for me.

As part of this different life I have been given, I have gotten to know many other families who deal with special needs and disabilities. I find that some of their stories are raw and wrought with difficulty. Yet even in the utter agony of the most difficult situations, God's powerful hand is at work. Within those stories I see my own life. I realize that though the fog of difficulty weighs me down and I feel like God could not be working through my pain, indeed, he is.

It is a great blessing when God allows us to see his power, presence, and purpose in our earthly lives and especially in the unexpected and difficult things we face. I have found that in the difficult times, the stories of others who have walked a similar path and lived to tell the story can be so helpful to me. It is especially helpful to me when they share the thread that runs through their stories. When I see that woven into every story is evidence of God's work and presence within the difficulties, I take heart. I am reminded that we serve a gracious and loving and ever-present God. The Bible tells us, "'My grace is sufficient for you, for my power is made perfect in weakness.' Therefore I will boast all the more gladly about my weaknesses, so that Christ's power may rest on me" (2 Corinthians 12:9), and this is so true in the lives of special-needs families.

It is my goal that you will identify with these families and their lives. Beyond identifying with them, I pray that you will be encouraged by God's presence, strength, and purpose throughout their journeys. As you see him in their stories, I hope you will take heart. He is in your story too. He loves you and your child so much that he sent his Son for you. The journey may not be easy, but he is with you and for you.

CHAPTER 2

How Will This Be?

SAMANTHA'S STORY

"'How will this be,' Mary asked the angel, 'since I am a virgin?'" (Luke 1:34).

When the angel Gabriel came to Mary to announce that she would be the mother of the Savior, Mary's response was a simple logistical question. "How will this be?" Mary knew how reproduction worked. She knew that because she was a virgin it wasn't humanly possible to be having a baby. Mary also knew that with God all things are possible. She was merely asking how. Because the angel was a representative of God, Mary was really asking God, "How will this be?"

Of course, God had an answer. He knew how it would be, how his plans would come to pass. When we ask God that same question, "How will this be?" we can be sure he knows the answer for us too.

❤ SAMANTHA'S STORY ❤

When I was pregnant with my second child, I automatically had a level 2 ultrasound because of family health history, and it was at that moment that my life and my faith drastically changed.

The perinatologist informed my husband and me that our child had a recessed chin. This was concerning because usually this is a result of a chromosomal abnormality. None of the possible abnormalities that were discussed with us were good. *How will this be, dear God? How?* We were scheduled for another ultrasound a week later.

After a week of waiting, our next ultrasound brought more concerning news. Our baby's abdomen was small in comparison to the rest of her body. She was diagnosed with IGR, which is intrauterine growth restriction. Eventually the baby's brain would stop growing because the abdomen was so small that it was not supplying enough nutrients to the brain. When this happened, the doctors would have to deliver our baby. *How will this be, dear God? How?*

Along with that concern, the chin was still quite a problem. A recessed chin greatly affects the size of the baby's airway. At this time, we were given the news that we needed to try to maintain the pregnancy until 32 weeks gestation for our child to have a viable chance at life. *How will this be, dear God? How?*

The doctors had to prepare me for a different kind of delivery. It was suggested they might have to do an "exit strategy procedure." The baby's recessed chin could cause potential problems at birth if not enough oxygen is transported to her brain. An exit strategy procedure would consist of the doctors delivering the baby while I was under complete anesthesia in the OR. They would deliver only the head of the baby so that the baby would still be attached and receiving oxygen through the umbilical cord. While the head would be outside of my womb, they would be able to try to intubate a breathing tube or, in the worst case scenario, perform a tracheotomy. As we faced these problems at 24 weeks into my pregnancy, we prayed for our unborn child. "Yet if I speak, my pain is not relieved; and if I refrain, it does not go away. Surely, God, you have worn me out" (Job 16:6,7). *How will this be, dear God? How?*

At this time, my mother, my pillar and example of faith, reminded me of the passage from Jeremiah 1:5: "Before I formed you in the womb I knew you, before you were born I set you apart; I appointed you as a prophet to the nations." I held this verse so closely to my heart and always tried to remind myself that, no matter what, this child was a gift from my heavenly Father. For this I could be grateful! Not only was this child a gift from my heavenly Father, but so was my mom. She pointed me to the author of life and reassured me that he knew exactly how this would be. He had formed my darling child in my womb. He had plans and a purpose for her.

Over the course of the next few weeks, and then months, it became completely apparent to me that this was all in the Lord's hands. The baby continued to grow at a consistent rate. Eventually 32 weeks came and went, and as we approached our final month, it was decided that I would be able to go full-term and deliver the baby naturally. There was no indication to the doctors that an exit strategy procedure would be necessary. God knew just *how* this would happen. He had a plan all along.

❤ ❤ ❤

It became completely apparent to me that this was all in the Lord's hands.

The Lord blessed my husband and me with our precious baby girl whom we named Olivia Grace. She only needed about one hour of oxygen and no other interventions. At birth, we discovered that she had a cleft palate. The cleft palate eventually led us to a diagnosis of a rare genetic syndrome called Emanuel syndrome (ES).

We learned that having Emanuel syndrome meant that Olivia would have significant physical disabilities and severe cognitive delays. Many children with ES spend years learning to independently sit, stand, and walk. Many are nonverbal and communicate with just a few signs. Throughout her life, Olivia is likely to face many health challenges including seizures, feeding issues, heart problems, gastrointestinal issues, and kidney problems. *"How will this be?"*

The Lord carried me, my worries, and my fears on his shoulders and showed me the way. It's not to say that my journey was over because my daughter was delivered full-term and was breathing on her own; my journey had just begun. Olivia has been such a blessing to me and my faith in Christ Jesus. God planned Olivia Grace. He planned for me to be her mom. He knew just how this would be. My relationship with the Lord has blossomed, and I've found new meaning and strength within the Word of God. Each day is a struggle for me, for my sweet Olivia, and for our family, but I rest assured that God knows the hows of our tomorrows. In my heart, I focus on the promises that our Lord has made. I remind myself that he is here, right with us. He wants me to lean on him. When I forget or grow weak, he sends the blessing of my mom and other Christians to point me to his Word. "Trust in the LORD with all your heart and lean not on your own understanding; in all your ways submit to him, and he will make your paths straight" (Proverbs 3:5,6). We have a God who knows "How will this be?" and we can trust him, just as Mary did.

Samantha and Nick Weissenborn are the parents of two daughters. Their younger daughter, Olivia Grace, has Emanuel syndrome.

$$\bullet \quad\text{—}\quad \heartsuit \; \heartsuit \; \heartsuit \quad\text{—}\quad \bullet$$

Sent Away Empty

BARB'S STORY

$$\bullet \quad\text{————————————}\quad \bullet$$

"He has filled the hungry with good things but has sent the rich away empty" (Luke 1:53).

When Mary praised the God who had chosen her to be the mother of his Son, she talked about God's provision. Mary praised the provider-God who "has filled the hungry with good things" and "has sent the rich away empty." This is a beautiful song to an incredible provider, but I wonder if Mary thought of her praise song as she was in labor and couldn't find a place to stay. As Joseph knocked on door after door and was told, "No room, no room," did Mary praise the God who provides? As each pain assaulted her and she knew that her Savior-baby would come soon, did she praise the God who provides? As it seemed like Mary and Joseph were the ones being "sent away empty," did Mary still praise God?

We don't know if Mary praised at that moment or not, but we do know that God did provide! He didn't provide a fancy hotel or even a feather bed. He didn't provide a midwife or hospital room. God provided the perfect place for his plan. He provided a stable and a manger. They weren't pretty and they probably didn't smell fantastic, but they were the perfect place for the birth of Mary's child, the world's Savior. They were just what was needed for the eternity story of humankind. God provided for Mary and Joseph. Our provider-God also provided for us in that manger. He provided a way to heaven. That same God provides for our needs here on earth, even when we wonder if God is sending us away empty, even when we don't know how he will provide.

♥ BARB'S STORY ♥

I have a saying I frequently use with other parents walking the journey of serious chronic illness, disability, or special needs: "Just when you think you have it figured out, you don't have it figured out." It almost seems unjust that right when a mother adapts to managing certain aspects of her child's needs or diagnosis, life changes or a new phase is entered, representing uncharted territory for the family. Thankfully, even in the face of these changes, God continues to provide.

This was surely the case for my own precious family when I found myself pregnant with our third child. My pregnancy was high risk, and things became more challenging with every passing day. I was already the blessed mother of a typical five-year-old kindergartener and a two-year-old toddler with severe hemophilia.

Hemophilia is a genetic bleeding disorder where an individual does not produce one of several proteins necessary to form a stable clot. This is particularly dangerous because internal bleeding can occur undetected for hours, only being recognized when things have become grave. The standard of treatment is to administer the missing clotting factor intravenously three to four times per week. The cost is staggering, running from $3,000 per year in infancy to $300,000 per year in adulthood. To contain such costs while also normalizing life, parents are taught to give these IV infusions at home when their children are mere toddlers.

Our family was just beginning to "normalize," treating our son at home, when I unexpectedly became pregnant. We were so fearful of having another child with this diagnosis, especially since we had begun to adapt to a new life of not having to run to a hospital 30 miles away three times or more per week. It was difficult not to worry. What if we had more than one of these "million dollar" babies? How would we ever make ends meet? How would our provider-God give us earthly provision in this?

Males typically have hemophilia at a greater rate because it is a gender-linked disorder. God's first great act of mercy toward our family regarding this new pregnancy occurred when a genetic ultrasound revealed that the child I was carrying this time was a girl. We felt like we could breathe a sigh of relief and finally begin to enjoy the pregnancy once we knew we were unlikely to confront hemophilia in this new baby.

For a short two months we were able to exhale, looking forward to adding to our numbers in early June of the upcoming year. We found ourselves dreaming of all the precious miracles a new baby brings. Visions of soft, cuddly stuffed animals and downy clothing smelling of baby powder danced in our heads.

Our time at that rest stop of joy was short-lived as the pregnancy became tenuous toward the end of the fourth month. At first I thought I was imagining the premature labor pains. Yet, once hooked up to monitors, we discovered the contractions weren't all in my head.

I was told to stay off my feet as much as possible, lower my stress level, and not overdo. No one was ever able to cogently explain how the mother of a toddler and a preschooler was supposed to successfully accomplish these goals. It was extremely stressful, and a little boy who wanted to be picked up and carried everywhere surely didn't help. Ordinary life—shuttling small children around, doing laundry, making meals, and keeping our home clean while also caring for myself—seemed superhuman. *Was God sending us away empty? How would he provide?*

Once again, God's hand of mercy intervened. With family unable or unwilling to help, the Lord filled the void by sending armies of people from church to bring us meals throughout my final trimester of pregnancy. He sent me a new mentor to fortify me spiritually and point me to his Word during this tumultuous time. Friends also stepped up to help with my energetic youngsters. I don't know how we could have managed without the practical care God sent us at such a difficult time.

Meanwhile, the contractions became more frequent and greater in strength. Unfortunately, our son's bleeding disorder continued in its complexity. Without explanation, we suddenly began having difficulty with venous access of our son. The every-other-day intravenous treatment our boy required was going terribly wrong. We had to run him in to the local emergency room or to the children's hospital 30 miles away because of repeated failure when we tried to put the needle into his arm. It was beyond discouraging. After advancing to home treatment, we were back to the stress of not knowing when we might have to run to a hospital at a moment's notice. The setback felt like being painted into a corner. *Was God sending us away empty? How would he provide?*

It was beyond discouraging.

We discussed having a central venous access device put into our son surgically to manage his treatment. Yet we didn't know what we would do if he was hospitalized and I went into labor and delivered. I discussed this absolute quandary with my doctor, hoping she could help us. She cavalierly replied that if such a situation happened, I would come to the maternity ward while my husband managed my son at the children's hospital. This did not sound like an acceptable option to us. At a time when I was supposed to be lowering my stress, this only served to create an almost hopeless state of panicked desperation. *Was God sending us away empty? How would he provide?*

Thank God that our circumstances never have the final say!

I managed to carry our third child to within two weeks of my due date. While there were signs that she would have benefited from staying in utero longer, she was generally healthy at birth. My husband and I were both there to joyfully welcome her into the world.

The following day my husband returned to the hospital with my older daughter and son to meet their baby sister. Both kids held the baby and oogled over this precious, delicate new family member. We took the obligatory photos with our cherished family, now five strong. Praise to our God!

After enjoying a fast-food lunch in my room, my son drifted off in the hospital bed next to me. Upon waking, he began bleeding from both his nose and mouth. It was likely from something poking him in his mouth that we hadn't noticed during lunch. Seeing the frank, gushing blood was terribly upsetting to him, and it was obvious that we needed him to have an emergency infusion right then and there. At the same time, we were terrified to try because of our recent lack of successful access. *Was God sending us away empty? How would he provide?* "Though he slay me, yet will I hope in him" (Job 13:15).

With some quick problem-solving running through my mind, I had my husband buzz my nurse, asking if one of the NICU nurses down the hall might come and administer our son's IV infusion in this emergency. After speaking to her supervisor, my nurse returned saying that we would have to take him all the way down to the emergency room at the opposite end of the hospital, have our son admitted, and then that team could infuse him.

"There's no time!" I plainly stated, and shot into action.

With a gray, groggy, dismayed husband who was looking like he was the one who had just given birth, I set up my son's infusion right on the table in my hospital room. Still adorned in my standard-issue gown and disposable socks, I prepared to insert the IV needle into my toddler's arm as my nurse stood at the door to my room, her mouth agape. Within minutes I had the blessed flow of clotting factor coursing through my child's veins.

It was a miracle! This was the first time our son had been successfully infused without repeat attempts in months. Praise to our God!

Despite the convergence of calamities over those challenging months, God repeatedly made his presence known to us, as he has in the years since. Every time there was a new crisis or worry confronting us, his hand of rescue and care grabbed hold of ours. Even when things didn't transpire the way we wanted or hoped, his plan went forward, keeping us safely in the center of his will. Our family's story is living proof that while God does not promise us an absence of troubles, he is ever faithful to his vow to never leave us hopelessly alone to confront them. God was not sending us away empty. He continued to provide. "Do not be anxious about anything, but in every situation, by prayer and petition, with thanksgiving, present your requests to God. And the peace of God, which transcends all understanding, will guard your hearts and your minds in Christ Jesus" (Philippians 4:6,7).

Barb and Steve Dittrich are the parents of one son and two daughters. Their son has severe hemophilia.

♥ ♥ ♥

CHAPTER 4

Grief That Pierces the Soul

CARRIE'S STORY

"This child is destined to cause the falling and rising of many in Israel, and to be a sign that will be spoken against, so that the thoughts of many hearts will be revealed. And a sword will pierce your own soul too" (Luke 2:34,35).

"The angel went to her and said, 'Greetings, you who are highly favored!'" (Luke 1:28).

When the angel Gabriel came to Mary to announce that she would be the mother of Jesus, he called her "you who are highly favored." When I think of a highly favored daughter, I think of an extra-special girl treated with great kindness and even some partiality by her dad. I think of that favored daughter being given special gifts, talents, or advantages. I don't think of the favored child being told that she would be given difficulty and hardships. I don't think of a favored child being blessed with a son whose circumstances and early death would make her feel as though a sword had pierced her own soul. This gift does not seem like a great gift of love from a dear father. When I think of Mary's circumstances and what she would watch her son endure, I think that if I were Mary, I might prefer to NOT be the favored child!!! Yet we know that Mary did receive the greatest gift of her life in her baby son. Mary's baby son wasn't only soft and sweet and, amazingly, her own child. Mary's baby son was also her perfect Savior. Mary would live in heaven one day with God because of this Savior-son. So although her heart would ache and her soul would feel as though a sword had pierced it, she was indeed a favored child of her God.

I think that physical, gut-wrenching, incapacitating pain is what the Bible meant when Mary heard the words "And a sword will pierce your own soul too." Sometimes in this life, our pain is so intense that it feels as though our very being, our soul, has been pierced with a sword. We feel the emotional pain as if it were a physical blow. It knocks the wind out of us. This is especially true when it involves our children.

And yet, even in the gut-wrenching pain, the Bible tells us that we too are highly favored and beloved children of God: "The LORD disciplines those he loves, as a father the son he delights in" (Proverbs 3:12). Notice those words "delights in." This is the opposite of how we feel about our pains and trials: we feel they are proof that God has overlooked us, when they are, in fact, special evidence that we are God's beloved children, that he delights in us.

While God blesses his children abundantly in this earthly life with spiritual and earthly blessings, he doesn't promise his beloved children an easy earthly life. In fact, the Bible tells us the opposite: "In this world you will have trouble. But take heart! I [Jesus] have overcome the world" (John 16:33).

♥ CARRIE'S STORY ♥

Our new baby was due Christmas Day. Since each of our five boys had been born three days early, I assumed this baby would come just before Christmas. I looked forward to celebrating the birth of Mary's Savior-son with my own newborn in my arms.

I was a little nervous about my 20-week ultrasound, but it went smoothly. With each of my other pregnancies, my 20-week ultrasounds had produced some questions or concerns that warranted a follow-up ultrasound. In fact, with my previous pregnancy the technician was concerned about a possible cyst on the brain and a cleft lip. We had followed up with a level 2 ultrasound, which showed a healthy baby—no cysts or cleft lip. So with this pregnancy, I repeatedly questioned if everything looked okay. I was reassured that everything looked beautiful.

Christmas came and went without the arrival of our baby. New Year's came and went too. Sometime during those weeks, the chain on my necklace broke from my little ones pulling on it. It feels weird for me to be without a necklace, so I reached for one with a sturdy chain—it was my Jeremiah 29:11 necklace: "'I know the plans I have for you,' declares the LORD, 'plans to prosper you and not to harm you, plans to give you hope and a future.'"

As I studied it, I was a little reluctant to put it on. It's a great passage, but one that is used often during hard times. The thought crossed my mind that it might portend something bad about the birth. I shrugged it off as a silly worry and put my necklace on.

The day after New Year's, I woke up feeling a little crampy. Only an hour or so later, our sweet Evangeline made a quick arrival. I remember some of my first thoughts when she was born. After having five boys, I was a little shocked that she was a girl. I also felt confused about her small size. She was over a week late and still a tiny 6.5 pounds. Each of my boys had weighed 8 to 9 pounds. I knew what a newborn cry should sound like, and Eva's sounded weaker than it should have. The nurses were giving Eva oxygen, but they claimed it wasn't because of anything too concerning—just the very quick delivery. Later, as I held Eva, I noticed that she had long pinkies and clenched hands that looked a little bit different than my boys' had. I was quietly noticing these things and some other differences about our new baby while trying hard to convince myself that nothing was amiss. I asked some nurses, but they evaded the question by saying what a beautiful baby I had.

As I held our new daughter, my husband was on the phone announcing Eva's arrival to friends and family. He told them that although she currently needed a little bit of help with oxygen, our little Eva would be just fine. As the beloved of the Father, we know this is absolutely true, yet we had no idea what the next few days and hours would bring and how important it would be for us to cling to that.

We had a wonderful pediatrician, but she didn't have visiting rights for the hospital where Eva was born. This meant that the hospital's on-call pediatrician visited us. We met this doctor for the first time when he examined Eva and then rambled for what seemed like 15 minutes about things that could possibly be wrong with our sweet, new daughter. When he finished his litany of possibilities, he asked if we had any questions. I was reeling. QUESTIONS?! I had just given birth to a baby who came quickly, but whose labor went the way labors are supposed to. My husband had just told our family and friends that our daughter would be fine. Now this pediatrician was telling me all sorts of shocking medical possibilities—things I hadn't ever thought of or considered—about my precious daughter! How could I even think of questions? I just needed to leave to go cry.

♥ ♥ ♥

When he finished his litany of possibilities, he asked if we had any questions. I was reeling.

I began to digest it. There was something horribly wrong with my little Eva. Nobody seemed to know quite what. Eva's body seemed to function properly except that she was having trouble sucking. So many scenarios were going through my head. *"And a sword will pierce your own soul too."*

When you pass through the waters, I will be with you; and when you pass through the rivers, they will not sweep over you. When you walk through the fire, you will not be burned; the flames will not set you ablaze. For I am the LORD your God, the Holy One of Israel, your Savior." (Isaiah 43:2,3)

Since she had some elevated white blood cell counts, the doctors decided to put Evangeline on IV antibiotics, which meant she would have to stay at the hospital for a week. This wasn't great news for us. We felt anxious to go home, introduce the boys to their baby sister, and get back to some normalcy.

We were hoping to have a church baptism that Sunday. The boys had memorized a song called "God's Own Child, I Gladly Say It." They had a violin and piano arrangement for it ready, and we planned for them to be a part of the baptism service. It would have been a beautiful way for our family to welcome our newest baby as a child of our God. Unfortunately, we were told that Eva would not be discharged from the hospital until Monday. So our plans would have to change.

The hospital staff told us we could use a big room in the hospital's lower level to have a baptism with a small number of loved ones. Again, we learned that God's plans and ours were not the same. On Sunday morning, a nurse checked Eva's blood oxygen level using a pulse oximeter on her finger and her toe and found they didn't match. This led the nurse to suspect a heart problem. I was informed that Eva needed to be transferred to Children's Hospital of Wisconsin, which was an hour away, and she needed to be transferred quickly.

I felt devastated. I had the beautiful baptismal gown that my mom had handmade and each of my children had worn ready for Eva to wear. I had a pretty cross necklace that was a gift from her godmother. Instead, I had to call my pastor-husband in the middle of church to inform him that our daughter might be on the verge of death!

The nurses on the floor assured my husband that it would take a couple of hours before the ambulance would come to transfer Eva, so we could still do a quick baptism with some relatives. The family came right after church, and Eva was baptized in a diaper with no special gown or special music. The tears and the frightened family members and ruined plans didn't change the power of Baptism and its promises for the littlest of children. Eva's baptism would be a powerful memory for us in the coming months. Yet for me, it felt like such a dark day. *"And a sword will pierce your own soul too."*

Although the children's hospital that Eva was transferred to was an hour from home, it was only minutes from my parents' house where the rest of our family could stay. Earthly supports like my parents and the close proximity of their house reassured us of God's presence and his provision for our family. Small provisions like this can be such a huge reminder in tough circumstances that we are the beloved of our Father, and we truly appreciated knowing that our boys were well cared for and nearby while we were at Eva's side.

Eva was examined at the children's hospital, and the staff quickly assured us that while she had a small hole in her heart, it wasn't gravely concerning and might even close on its own in a couple of years. Eva had only needed oxygen for a day right after she was born. She had been breathing on her own until her transfer. During her hospital transfer, she screamed nonstop for the entire ambulance ride. After that, she was never able to wean herself from the oxygen again. Her problems sucking were also very concerning.

While Eva had been in Waupun, no one had been able to get a good blood draw from her. Our wonderful pediatrician (who, as I mentioned before, did not have rights at the hospital) visited Eva "as a friend" and was able to draw blood. The results of those tests came back two days after we arrived at Children's. The woman who gave us the test results was crying before she gave them to us. Our Eva had trisomy 18. This diagnosis was very grim. It meant that Eva would likely die before her first birthday—and if not, she would have very severe disabilities. Thinking of such a different and scary future was so very difficult and painful. *"And a sword will pierce your own soul too."*

This period was a huge crisis in my life. Would I love this baby like my healthy, typical ones? Would she require daily, constant care for my whole life? Would I ever go on vacation again? How could I care for my other children properly if Eva was going to have significant needs? And then I thought, *What is wrong with me? My husband and boys already adore and love this baby unconditionally, and I have all these horrible thoughts?* I asked myself if I had really wanted some sort of a superbaby. Had I wanted a child that would be cute? Did I want a daughter who would learn to read before age 3? Was it important to me that she excel on a musical instrument? In truth, I may have hoped for some incredible talents, but mostly I had just wanted a "normal" baby. I expected a "normal" baby. What if Eva never smiled or never gave any indication that she cared about me at all—how could I cope with that? Again, I thought, *What is wrong with me????* Of course my post-pregnancy hormones were all going crazy. I felt bad that I wasn't helping with my two-year-old who was missing Mommy so much. I missed my other boys and knew how much they each depended on me and needed me. Yet I felt that I needed to be with my daughter to care for her and feed her. I was being pulled in so many directions!

♥ ♥ ♥

Thankfully, my thoughts, born of hurt and confusion and fear, didn't change my Father's love.

One night I stopped at my parents' house for an hour or so. My dad asked me what I was thinking. I remember saying that I just wanted it to be over. It seemed easier if Eva would just die. I felt horrible for saying it and even more so for thinking it. Yet that is what I, the beloved of my Father, thought about the daughter he had gifted to me. Thankfully, my thoughts, born of hurt and confusion and fear, didn't change my Father's love.

Despite the fact that most trisomy babies have major organ problems, Eva didn't. She was bigger than most as well. Because of her relative good health, it seemed possible that Eva could live a long time. We were also told that she was likely deaf or very hard of hearing. Doctors didn't know if she could see well. I wondered how, with my perfectionist tendencies, I would be able to deal with this. And while I kept crying out to God and reading my Bible, the tears just kept coming and the sadness wasn't going away. *"And a sword will pierce your own soul too."*

The staff at Children's wanted to send us home soon, and we were eager to go home too. In order for us to do this, they gave us three options for Eva's feeding. Option 1: We could use the feeding tube down her nose as we had been. I would pump breast milk and then pour the milk down her throat every three hours. Option 2: We could have surgery to place a G-tube. Eva might not survive the surgery, and we'd have to stay in the hospital for a long recovery. Option 3: We could just nourish her as best we could through bottles and nursing and eventually she wouldn't get enough nutrition and would pass away. This would not be painful or cause her to suffer. We were reassured over and over that all three options were okay. In the end, we chose the first option. We wanted to nourish our daughter as best as we could without the danger of surgery. Letting her starve wasn't an option to us.

As we prepared to leave the hospital, we were encouraged to have lots of death plans—when we would resuscitate, when we would not, etc. Who would have ever thought we'd be doing this for our newborn?

As we headed home with our whole family together, we were happy—so happy to be together, finally! Those were some of the best days. God lifted me out of the fog of depression. Many friends and relatives came to meet Eva. The boys begged to hold their little sister all the time. Though I was exhausted with all her appointments, pumping, feeding every three hours, and never getting more than two hours of consecutive sleep, I was happy. I was growing to love my little girl. So many, many people showed they cared. It is the love of God's people on earth sometimes that reminds us of how beloved we are to our Father. It is their arms around us and their tears with us that show us a tiny hint of his incredible love for us.

Our pediatrician visited our home weekly so that Eva wouldn't be exposed to more germs in the office. A home nurse came every couple days to check on us. They were so encouraging to me.

One of my favorite times was prayer time. When my family came together and prayed—it was a powerful time of encouragement as the Holy Spirit worked to strengthen and reassure my battered heart and grow the faith within. During Eva's life, and for a time after, I could not say the words to "Now I Lay Me Down to Sleep" without crying. Now that the starkness of the situation has been made less intense by time, this prayer doesn't always move me to tears. However, I find that its meaning is so much more real now.

My worship life also changed. The meaning of hymns in church touches my tender heart in ways that it didn't before. There are many hymns that I have sung my entire life. It is only since having Eva that I realize how many hymns speak of death. When I would go to church with Eva, it was impossible not to think about the depth of meaning in the songs. She would be lying in my lap as I sang, and I wondered how much time I might have with my little daughter. Every hymn had new meaning to me.

I had a fear about Eva's death—how it would happen and how I would react. Even in death, God was gracious. I awoke one night and couldn't hear the normal Eva sounds. When I picked up my darling baby, I could tell she wasn't breathing. My little girl was gone. I woke Topher and he cried, "I prayed, Carrie." We held her for awhile and let her brothers hold her if they wanted, though most didn't since she was cold. Perhaps it was being overtired, perhaps it was because we had been told over and over again she would die, but the thought never even crossed our minds to try CPR—I don't know if it would have had any effect or not.

Just the night before, as I had been giving her and some of my other little ones a bath, one of the boys had asked how old I thought Eva would be when she died. I had just murmured something like, "I don't know." He had replied, "I think she'll live to be 86!"

The next days and weeks were some of the hardest. Even though God had been gracious in the way he had taken our Eva, it still was not easy. I woke up at 2:40 each night for the next few months—the same time I had woken and found her unresponsive. And naturally, it wasn't easy to get back to sleep. I kept myself busy caring for my family, but whenever I had a moment of rest, the heartache was overwhelming. *"And a sword will pierce your own soul too."*

But the hardest part of all was the grave. The winter of 2011–2012 was a very mild one. Only three days were notably snowy: the day we brought Eva home from the hospital, the day she died, and the day we buried her. Burying my daughter was the most horrible thing I have ever done in my life. I took my little girl, put her in a box, placed her in the cold, hard ground, and left her there. My head knows my daughter was really not in that body, but my heart doesn't. That's the little body that grew inside me, the cheeks I pressed against my own, the little person I snuggled and rocked and loved. As unrealistic as it was, I really just wanted to keep her lifeless body with me forever. My husband took comfort in visting her grave often to be with her, but I didn't really want to have any part of the memory of the grave. I'm not sure I'll ever be able to think of the grave and my daughter without a horrid ache in my heart and tears pouring down my cheeks. I take comfort in picturing her in heaven, with Jesus snuggling her little body, but the grave's sting is still so potent.

Do you remember the song that I said my children had prepared for their sister's baptism but had never been able to sing then? Their singing and violin and piano playing beautified Eva's funeral instead. The words were so very fitting:

> God's own child, I gladly say it:
> I am baptized into Christ!
> He, because I could not pay it,

Gave my full redemption price.
Do I need earth's treasures many?
I have one worth more than any
That brought me salvation free,
Lasting to eternity!

Sin, disturb my soul no longer:
I am baptized into Christ!
I have comfort even stronger:
Jesus' cleansing sacrifice.
Should a guilty conscience seize me
Since my baptism did release me
In a dear forgiving flood,
Sprinkling me with Jesus' blood?

Satan, hear this proclamation:
I am baptized into Christ!
Drop your ugly accusation;
I am not so soon enticed.
Now that to the font I've traveled,
All your might has come unraveled,
And, against your tyranny,
God, my Lord, unites with me!

Death, you cannot end my gladness:
I am baptized into Christ!
When I die, I leave all sadness
To inherit paradise!
Though I lie in dust and ashes
Faith's assurance brightly flashes:
Baptism has the strength divine
To make life immortal mine.

There is nothing worth comparing
To this lifelong comfort sure!
Open-eyed my grave is staring:
Even there I'll sleep secure.
Though my flesh awaits its raising,
Still my soul continues praising:
I am baptized into Christ;
I'm a child of paradise!

As time has gone on, God has been faithful and has reassured me in his Word that he is my Father and I am his beloved. I have struggled with my prayer life in the years since Eva's death, and God continues to help me as I struggle.

Shortly after Eva's death we were able to e-mail and share encouragement with two different families who were facing the loss of their babies. We were able to share encouragements from God's Word and be with them in their pain. We also took a family vacation to Faith's Lodge—a place where people gather to share comfort over children who have died or are very sick. Over time our family has been able to witness Jesus' love as he has comforted us through songs and prayers and togetherness. As we live our life as Eva's family, but without our Eva here on earth, we appreciate when we can see eternal purpose, and our hurting hearts are soothed a bit.

I'm sure God has given me a depth of compassion that I did not have before I became Eva's mom. Do I know that in making me Eva's mom God grew my faith, my compassion, and my gratitude for what he's given me? Yes. Would I still ever be strong enough to pick such a struggle for myself? I doubt it. But I hope he keeps growing my faith so that someday I can truthfully say I would be happy with any struggle he gives me that will further his kingdom.

I know that I am God's beloved because I know my faithful Father from his Word. I am so thankful that my circumstances have never changed who he is and how beloved I am to him.

Carrie Doerr and her husband, Topher, are the parents of six boys and one girl. Their daughter, Evangeline, was born with trisomy 18.

CHAPTER 5

Where Is God's Mighty Hand?

"JANE'S" STORY

"He has performed mighty deeds with his arm; he has scattered those who are proud in their inmost thoughts. He has brought down rulers from their thrones but has lifted up the humble" (Luke 1:51,52).

"An angel of the Lord appeared to Joseph in a dream. 'Get up,' he said, 'take the child and his mother and escape to Egypt. Stay there until I tell you, for Herod is going to search for the child to kill him.' So he got up, took the child and his mother during the night and left for Egypt, where he stayed until the death of Herod. And so was fulfilled what the Lord had said through the prophet: 'Out of Egypt I called my son.' When Herod realized that he had been outwitted by the Magi, he was furious, and he gave orders to kill all the boys in Bethlehem and its vicinity who were two years old and under, in accordance with the time he had learned from the Magi. Then what was said through the prophet Jeremiah was fulfilled:

'A voice is heard in Ramah,
weeping and great mourning,
Rachel weeping for her children
and refusing to be comforted,
because they are no more'"
(Matthew 2:13-18).

I wonder what Mary was thinking as she escaped to Egypt with her husband and baby son. She and Joseph obviously trusted God or they wouldn't have gone. I wonder, though, if there was even a small part of her weak human heart that quietly wondered why.

We have already read how just after Mary learned that she would be the mother of the Savior, she praised God, saying, "He has performed mighty deeds with his arm; he has scattered those who are proud in their inmost thoughts. He has brought down rulers from their thrones but has lifted up the humble. He has filled the hungry with good things but has sent the rich away empty. He has helped his servant Israel, remembering to be merciful to Abraham and his descendants forever, just as he promised our ancestors" (Luke 1:51-55). Why did Mary sing about all of that? Having grown up in a God-fearing home, these were the kinds of things she had been taught that the Savior was coming to do. She and her fellow Jewish believers were expecting the Savior to topple the wicked from their thrones, to undo poverty and starvation, to send the oppressors into homelessness, etc. In fact, the victories Jesus ended up winning were bigger and longer-lasting, and the thrones he toppled included the one Satan himself had ruled from for so long.

I can't help but wonder: as she and Joseph prepared to escape with their baby son, or later as she heard about babies being killed, did she think back to those words of praise? Herod killing babies and threatening Mary's Savior-son seemed like the very opposite of the proud being scattered or wicked rulers being dethroned. It seemed like the sheer abandonment of those who love God.

❤ ❤ ❤

It seemed like the very opposite of the proud being scattered or wicked rulers being dethroned.

Don't we sometimes look around our broken world and wonder where our almighty God is in the midst of this? We know God and that he is always loving and always worthy. We know that his history in Scripture shows us this. In our weakness, though, we look around our world and we might wonder. We see the proud living in big homes. We see them having healthy child after healthy child, and we sure don't see them stopping to thank God for these blessings. It looks to us like others are being rewarded with success upon success. We look around and see abundance and waste in our country full of great riches. We see greed and deceit and lack of appreciation. We see the American poor, and we read of the great poverty in other countries. We know that so many are hungry and wanting. We know that many are unloved and uncared for in our world. We cannot turn on a television or computer without hearing of war and terrorism and hate. We might think, "Why does our good, almighty God allow all of that to happen?" We might read

Mary's song and think why. Where is the God who promised to help his servant Israel? Where is the God who promises to help me? Where is his strong arm? Why doesn't he show me his mighty hand?

Mary knew that she trusted in a God who had done mighty and miraculous things throughout history. Yet that same God did not topple Herod. The God who split the waters for the Israelites, the God who tumbled the walls of Jericho, the God who enabled a little boy to fell a giant with a small stone—this amazing God allowed an evil ruler to kill so many small babies. This amazing God allowed such heartache. This amazing God allowed so many mothers to be struck with an aching hole in their hearts for the rest of their earthly lives.

After her incredibly lowly birthing experience, I wonder what Mary thought as she had to flee with her baby and her husband. First such a lowly birth and now this?! When she learned of the fate of so many babies, I wonder how Mary's prayers to God sounded. Did she ever ask, "Why doesn't he show me his mighty hand?"

❤ "JANE'S" STORY ❤

My son "Daniel" has autism. When he was young, the general public didn't have an understanding of autism the way they do today. I was working hard every day to get the services that Daniel needed (even when I wasn't quite sure what he needed, just something!!!) and the best education for him. I was often judged harshly by the people around me. I think that people often looked at

Daniel and figured that a boy his age was old enough to behave certain ways. His behavior was always different than what they expected. When his behavior didn't fit into their idea of acceptable, they just assumed that I was being a lenient mom. This was true throughout his childhood, and it never made things easy for our family or for him.

At one point in our lives, this even meant that our family wasn't welcome in worship. We would go to church, and the sensory stimuli were overwhelming to Daniel—bright lights, too hot, too cold, lots of people, high ceilings, loud music, loud pastor, everyone standing, everyone sitting, everyone singing, everyone talking in unison. It was too much. He would make noises or climb under the pews. He was far too big for this to be typical behavior, but instead of trying to understand or offering help to our family, we were made to feel unwelcome. We got bad looks and stares. Finally, a fellow worshiper unkindly asked us to make our son behave. After that we took a break from church. Sometimes things are so hard that we wonder, "Why doesn't God show me his mighty hand?" Although my feelings of hurt and rejection over this were intense, I continued to talk to God and to seek his will for our family. I also continued to attend the women's Bible study at our church.

Daniel's behavior became more and more difficult as he got older. There were many days when I felt like giving up, especially during middle school. Things continued to spiral downward until we finally had to check Daniel into a treatment center. It was the most difficult thing that we have ever done. *Why does my almighty God allow all of this?*

At the treatment center, Daniel was taught one-on-one by a teacher who truly wanted to understand him. He also started meeting with our pastor every week. This was the beginning of real healing and progress for our family and Daniel. I truly think it was a turning point.

Daniel and the pastor studied the Word together, and as they did, our pastor noticed that Daniel had a very good understanding of God's Word. Over time the pastor realized that he needed some help in dealing with some of Daniel's behaviors, so he contacted Jesus Cares Ministries. A man named Bill from Jesus Cares took over meeting with Daniel to study God's Word. Bill also became a close friend of Daniel's and an incredible Christian mentor to him. Daniel is able to live his faith and share it in such beautiful ways as he learns to become more independent in his life. Bill helps Daniel navigate the difficulties of everyday life by being his friend and spending time with him. His example and advice are huge in Daniel's life. Bill continues to study God's Word with Daniel, and they draw closer to the Lord together. When I look at the ways Daniel has developed since his time at the treatment center, I can see that God has used it for such good.

God's grace and purpose in Daniel's life was also evident to me in his friendship with "Kyle." Kyle was a boy that Daniel met at school. Kyle was legally blind in one eye and had been sick with cancer for a number of years.

Kyle's home life was hard, and his mom wasn't around all that much. Kyle came home with Daniel often and really became a part of our family's life. We celebrated Kyle's birthdays, made sure he was always fed, and tried to fill in where Kyle's mom sometimes lacked. To be honest, we were very happy to have Kyle in our lives since Daniel hadn't had a lot of friends through his school years. We were excited for Daniel to have a good friend, and we welcomed him! Our family often shared Jesus' love with Kyle, and Daniel was especially excited to share news about his Savior with his friend.

Unfortunately, Kyle just disappeared one day. He didn't come to school, and the apartment he had shared with his mom was empty. He had moved away without a good-bye.

After leaving without a good-bye and hearing nothing for a year, I got a call from Kyle's mom. She had grim news. The cancer was severe and they didn't expect Kyle to live very long. They were now living far away from our Wisconsin home—in Indiana—and she said that Kyle very much wanted to see Daniel. Kyle was important to all of us, so I made arrangements for Daniel and me to visit him. Knowing that Kyle's time on earth was short, Daniel looked forward to the visit because he wanted to share Jesus with his friend. The visit went well.

Kyle continued to ask for Daniel, and Daniel often had a desire to visit Kyle, so we went back several times. Whenever we went to visit, Daniel spent his time sharing Jesus and the hope of heaven with Kyle. Kyle listened eagerly. During one of our visits, Kyle passed away while Daniel was with him.

We attended Kyle's funeral, and amidst the sadness, Kyle's grandfather came up to me and thanked me for encouraging Daniel's friendship with Kyle. He thanked me for bringing Daniel to visit so regularly. He said that Daniel was the best thing that ever happened to Kyle and talked happily about the joy that Kyle had as he looked forward to the hope of heaven—a hope he hadn't known prior to Daniel sharing Jesus with him. He expressed the feeling that Kyle was a different person—one with happiness and hope—after hearing about Jesus.

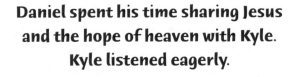

Daniel spent his time sharing Jesus and the hope of heaven with Kyle. Kyle listened eagerly.

My heart burst with thanksgiving to God. There was another soul spending eternity in paradise and God had used my son, my Daniel, as a tool in his kingdom! My boy's purpose was evident. Right here! What a blessing to know that this son whom I had worked so hard and fought so long for—this son whom I had prayed over and begged God to help me with, this son who had seemed so troubled and difficult at times—was truly full of God's purpose. I knew this. God had told me in his Word. Jeremiah 29:11-13 says, "'I know the plans I have for you,' declares the LORD, 'plans to prosper you and not to harm you, plans to give you hope and a future. Then you will call on me and come and pray to me, and I will listen to you. You will seek me and find me when you seek me with all your heart.'" For years and years I had been discouraged by what others said about my Daniel. It was such a blessing to hear about how he had truly been God's tool in sharing Jesus with Kyle! God doesn't always let us see what he is doing with hard situations. It was such an amazing blessing to be able to see this in Daniel and Kyle's relationship.

By God's grace, I am able to trust God's plans even though I don't always understand them. I know that his will is perfect. Daniel has now been confirmed. He has a job at Goodwill and is learning sign language. I praise God for all of the progress he makes every day, but I especially thank God for the ways that Daniel's faith allows him to reach out to others. I never would have imagined that this was possible! Daniel's genuine desire to help others brings me to tears at times. His heart for the Lord is truly beautiful. His dream for the future is to serve the Lord as a volunteer through Jesus Cares Ministries. He hopes to live in a group home someday. I truly believe that by the grace of God, Daniel will be able to do these things, and I thank God for allowing me to see the incredible ways he is using my son to touch others with the gospel.

This mother and family have chosen to remain anonymous, so the names have been changed. All other information is factual.

❤ ❤ ❤

CHAPTER 6

Why Have You Treated Us Like This?

JOANNA'S STORY

"Every year Jesus' parents went to Jerusalem for the Festival of the Passover. When he was twelve years old, they went up to the festival, according to the custom. After the festival was over, while his parents were returning home, the boy Jesus stayed behind in Jerusalem, but they were unaware of it. Thinking he was in their company, they traveled on for a day. Then they began looking for him among their relatives and friends. When they did not find him, they went back to Jerusalem to look for him. After three days they found him in the temple courts, sitting among the teachers, listening to them and asking them questions. Everyone who heard him was amazed at his understanding and his answers. When his parents saw him, they were astonished. His mother said to him, 'Son, why have you treated us like this? Your father and I have been anxiously searching for you'" (Luke 2:41-48).

Mary and Joseph searched and searched all day. In a strange town they looked for their young son. He was on the cusp of adulthood, but he was still a boy—12 years old. As a parent it is natural for me to imagine how I might have felt in their shoes. Mary was anxious. Was it so extreme that it gave Mary a bellyache as she rushed from place to place searching for her son? Did all of this tension give way to anger at some point? When Mary finally found Jesus, her question to him, "Why have you treated us like this?" echoes what we sometimes feel about Jesus.

♥ JOANNA'S STORY ♥

I had a very bright firstborn who was ahead of the curve on every milestone. She was early to walk, early to talk, early to potty train, early to read. I was a very proud mother, and I wanted another feather in my cap. When I had my second daughter, to my shock she wasn't ahead of the curve. In fact, Eden never hit any milestones. At four months, she was found to have "failure to thrive." Nystagmus (a ticking of the eyes) was noticed, which indicated a neurological disorder. Eden had other vision issues, mitochondrial issues, poor muscle tone, auditory processing problems, and sensory defensive disorder. She was able to hold her head up at seven months.

Around that time it was determined that Eden had an undiagnosed genetic disorder and was globally developmentally delayed. She learned to sit up at one and a half years old. At that time she started intensive therapy at the center for the blind. She began walking at three and a half years old. Also at three and a half, Eden was definitively diagnosed with a genetic condition: chromosome 16 duplication. Neither my husband nor I had it. It was a fluke that must have happened at conception. When we face things like this, it can be our human nature to ask Jesus, *"Why have you treated us like this?"*

Because of chromosome 16 duplication, Eden has symptoms of severe autism and is developmentally delayed. She doesn't play with peers. She is mute—I have never heard her voice. She is very emotionally aloof. Eden has had problems with wandering off and escaping, and we have had to call the police more than once to help us find her. She communicates with a few signs, a communication device, and some picture cards. At present, she enjoys touching water, hearing music, and learning, and I know she loves being loved.

Eden feels so frustrated, so often. She is stuck inside of a broken body. She can't communicate easily with this body and, sadly, often becomes angry and aggressive in her frustrations. Sometimes when I see her anger and pain, I ask Jesus, *"Why have you treated us like this?"*

A few weeks ago, my youngest daughter, Charlize, fell off her high chair and I ran to her and scooped her up. I tried to comfort her under the table while she cried hysterically. When Eden heard this, she was so overwhelmed by the sound of Charlize's cries. Eden doesn't understand how to manage her emotions. Screaming in her own frustration, Eden ran over to us and started pulling Charlize's hair and head-butting Charlize to get her to stop crying. I tried to push her away and pull us out from under the table. My oldest daughter, Zanna, saw our distress and wanted to help. Zanna ran over and tried pulling Eden away. Eden then turned and started pulling Zanna's hair and trying to bite her head. There we were—a big pile of girls screaming under the table. Thankfully my husband was able to come to our rescue and help get things under control. *Oh, Jesus, "Why have you treated us like this?"*

—— ♥ ♥ ♥ ——

In my aloneness, I ran ragged trying to find the fix—the magic cure.

When everything first started to transpire, I found myself grieving. I was grieving the loss of normal—the loss of the family I always pictured. But my husband wasn't grieving. He thought Eden would outgrow whatever this was. He didn't want to think about it, and he didn't want to talk about it. It seemed to make others feel awkward to talk about it. I was grieving alone. I hated my situation. I hated the isolation it brought, hated my family being different, hated all the work. At times, I even felt like I hated Eden, and I had even told her so, but she just stared blankly into the distance as she usually did. *Oh, Jesus, "Why have you treated us like this?"*

In my aloneness, I ran ragged trying to find the fix—the magic cure. I was in the rat race of not knowing what was wrong. I had to find that hidden cure. One nutritionist even told me that if I would give Eden X, Y, and Z, "She could end up as the valedictorian of her class one day." So there I was cracking coconuts, making homemade formula, and stuffing her full of every nutritional supplement that we could afford. I was completely mentally and emotionally broken. *Oh, Jesus, "Why have you treated us like this?"*

One summer day when she was three, before she was walking or feeding herself, I was spoon-feeding Eden lunch and, though it often felt like day in, day out drudgery to get her to eat, this day I felt such a joy in my spirit as I did it. So I grabbed a piece of paper and wrote on it,

> I have to remember that God has so much value for Eden. Don't see her worth through the eyes of the world. She has no worth in their eyes, but in the Father's eyes, she is deeply loved and adored and noticed.
>
> Don't see that God put her in my life to teach me a lesson, but see that God put me in her life to care for her. If he were here, he'd feed her every day, but he wants me to be his hands and care for her.
>
> She has so much value to him. He is so much more impressed by children than adults, and her childish innocence will always be there.
>
> Christ said, "Whatever you have done unto the least of the brethren, you have done it unto me." She is the least of the brethren. She has lower

worth in our society than even the poor and the orphaned. People want to abort her kind. The forever babies are the lowest.

It is perhaps not true that she was purposed this way for our family, but we were purposed for her.

If Jesus were here, in the flesh, he would heal her in a second because, though he allowed it, he didn't will that she be this way. Her dysfunction is a symptom of decay in this world. But regardless, every day I have the opportunity to work with the least of the brethren. Yes, whatever you have done unto the least of the brethren, you have done it unto Christ. And so everyday, I wash Jesus' hands and spoon-feed him meals and wipe up his messes and do therapy with him. I get to do that for Jesus.

So, I see that God has blessed me by bringing ministry into my home. When I was young, I had a great desire to do mission work. I'd leave church camp with that fire in my belly, thinking about going wherever God wanted me to serve him. Then I'd never really pursue it. Maybe it wasn't my calling to go far-off, or maybe I wasn't really willing. Maybe it's a fault in my personality—I'm not a planner. In the end, it doesn't matter. He brought the needy right into my home. My ministry is right here in serving my sweet daughter. I need not ask, *Oh, Jesus, "Why have you treated us like this?"*

Having Eden for our daughter was a blessing to my marriage. We had very intense marital problems. There were many times that I thought our marriage wouldn't survive. Certainly Eden's disability added a lot of strain to our marriage. Even deeper, though, her disability made it too difficult to get up and leave. We were stuck in our marriage because of Eden's needs. We had to hash it out—her needs were too complex to leave to just one of us. Families with autism have an 80 percent divorce rate. Ironically, for us, Eden's needs helped to preserve our marriage during its most difficult times.

It is a blessing to see beauty formed in my other two children that I never could have taught them with words. If I am at the grocery store with Zanna and we hear a child yelling in another aisle, neither of us turn to each other and say, "What a bad kid." Instead, Zanna has turned to me and said, "Mommy, that kid might have a disability." I see empathy and understanding for the needy in her.

In a strange way, I suppose it is a blessing that there are certain pains I'll never endure from Eden as a parent, the way I may with my other two children. Because she is mute I may never hear the words "I love you" from Eden's lips, but I'll also never hear her say angry words. I may never deal with a valedictorian, but I'll also never deal with a child choosing addiction or crimes, the way I may with my other two.

So I have come to see this in our family as a blessing—not that it is easy to live with day in and day out, but I have found hope from Christ in it all. Christ said, "Blessed is anyone who does not stumble on account of me" (Matthew 11:6). I see Eden's disability as one of the things he has allowed into my life to reveal my lack of trust in him and then grow it. Pain seems to have brought to the surface what I really believe about God. It exposed a scary choice I would have to make. Do I live with pain while believing "God is good," or do I fall away and say, "A good God would never allow this into my life," in which case, did I ever really trust him to begin with? *Oh, Jesus, "Why have you treated us like this?"* With the help of the Holy Spirit, God is growing my trust in him through these difficulties. God is still good. The drudgery of taking care of all of Eden's needs can feel like a curse. Yet when I see it as refining me and making me patient, kinder, more loving, and Christlike, I am set free to embrace what he has allowed and to accept this "new kind of normal."

Our pastor has been speaking on the Beatitudes on Sundays. A few weeks ago, he was speaking on "Blessed are those who mourn." He talked about John's description in Revelation of what heaven is like: heaven is without any suffering or pain. As I read and listened, my spirit welled up with excitement as I imagined my little Eden without her broken body. I used the pew Bible to look up the verse, and in the Bible, the heading to the passage on heaven said, "Eden Restored." My daughter's name— Restored. I cried with joy when I read it, and I felt God had it printed just for me.

Life is so short, and when I look at it from an eternal perspective, I see this difficulty so differently. I need not ask, *Oh, Jesus, "Why have you treated us like this?"* These momentary difficulties for me will be gone when this life is over, and one day, in heaven, Eden will meet with me and she'll look me in my eyes, smile at me, and I'll hear her lovely voice say words. Her voice will unite with mine to praise our God. Perhaps her voice will say, "Hello, Mommy, I love you."

Joanna and Sam Hughes are the parents of three daughters. Their second daughter, Eden, has chromosome 16 duplication.

CHAPTER 7

Anxiously Searching for the Lord

PAM'S STORY

"Your father and I have been anxiously searching for you" (Luke 2:48).

"Your father and I have been anxiously searching for you." It is easy for me to forget, when I'm reading this story, that every word Mary said to Jesus she was saying to her almighty God. Jesus' answer to Mary was, "Why were you searching for me? Didn't you know I had to be in my Father's house?" Mary and Joseph had been looking all day in the wrong places. When they finally looked in the right place, the Father's house, they found Jesus. He had been there all day long! As his parents had been searching the city, Jesus had been teaching and learning God's Word.

Have you ever wanted to say to God, "I have been anxiously searching for you"? Not because you couldn't physically locate him, but because you felt lost in the troubles of this world?

Maybe life has been hard for a long time and you are weary. Maybe there are disappointments that have been big. Because we are sinful, there are times when our sights aren't set on our Savior and the promise of heaven. We mistakenly let our focus dwell on earthly circumstances. These are times when we search and search in all of the wrong places for hope and purpose. We want answers and solutions and earthly satisfaction. We even pray and wonder WHY God doesn't answer us. We are looking for the answers that we want from God, and when we don't see them, we think that God hasn't answered us. Thankfully, God gives us his Word and Christian pastors, teachers, and loved ones to point us to his Son. Our faithful God is always near, and his love for us is unchanged by our distraction.

❤ PAM'S STORY ❤

When my children were young, I was anxiously searching. I was searching for a diagnosis and some concrete answers. You see, my second child, Noah, did not develop the way that his older sister had. Although we brought Noah home from the hospital and thought he was a healthy baby, he wasn't reaching developmental milestones as his older sister had. As time went on, we worried. We knew that something wasn't quite right, but we weren't sure what. We took Noah to see many specialists in search of a diagnosis. The doctors ran every type of test possible. Some of these tests were simple, but some were uncomfortable and invasive for Noah. We yearned for answers. We left no stone unturned, and yet there seemed to be no answers. Doctor after doctor and clinic after clinic sent us away without explanation. I prayed and prayed. Yet God seemed to remain silent. *"I have been anxiously searching for you."*

One of the many doctors whom we saw was a leading geneticist. She assured us that although she couldn't tell us why Noah had such delays and health struggles, she felt almost certain that it wasn't genetic. We had begun to think about and pray about having a third child. Becoming pregnant was never easy for us. Knowing this, I prayed that I would only become pregnant again if it was God's will. Imagine my surprise when I quickly conceived.

Noah was four when he became a big brother. His younger brother, Braden, was born healthy and had a fantastic Apgar score. We brought home our sweet newborn, but as Braden grew, we realized that he wasn't learning to track with his eyes or developing new skills as quickly as he should. We also noticed that he had an unusual amount of respiratory congestion. By three months old, we began to fear that Braden would have delays the way that Noah did.

**She felt almost certain
that it wasn't genetic.**

We continued our search during those early years of raising our small children. Daily life was filled with our daughter's activities and caring for Noah and baby Braden. Noah was sick and often required hospital stays. Braden was fairly healthy in those early years, but I can remember a time when both boys were hospitalized together. I had one sick little boy on each side of the hospital room. Can you imagine? Just thinking back, it is almost unimaginable. During that hospital stay, I remember that a pulmonary doctor came into the boys' room. He commented that it wouldn't be long before Braden ended up just like Noah— requiring a G-tube for feedings. I was so angry. It was hard enough having both of my boys in the hospital, but a doctor who predicted my son's future in such a negative way made it so much worse! *"I have been anxiously searching for you."*

After so much illness, Noah passed away a month shy of his sixth birthday. Although we had searched and searched, during Noah's lifetime we were never given an answer. We never knew why our son suffered. *"I have been anxiously searching for you."*

During Noah's life and those years of searching, I was a Christian. I knew Jesus, and I knew that through him salvation and an eternity in heaven were mine. Still, I was incredibly unhappy. I didn't like the way that my life had gone. I wanted things in life to go my way. I yearned to have healthy children who ran, played, jumped, yelled, whispered, talked, and so much more. I felt envy for parents who could pass the ball with their son in the yard. Sometimes when I was out driving, I would look at other houses and wonder what life was like inside of them. I felt sure that these families didn't have oxygen machines beeping from low saturations or feeding pumps beeping to signal the end of a cycle. I thought about how those homes definitely weren't filled with the sound of one-sided conversations as a parent places call after call to doctors and insurance companies and therapists to fight for her children's needs. Surely the people in those homes weren't fighting every day just to keep their child alive. Surely those houses were peaceful inside. I longed for a peaceful life. *"I have been anxiously searching for you."*

I rarely got to do the everyday things that parents with healthy kids were able to do. Noah was in the hospital so much. I was living at the hospital with him a good deal of time. I was fighting with my husband. Date nights didn't exist. Our conversations so often had to be about all of the management of care. (There was so much to manage!!!) I just wasn't content.

I cursed God and was angry and miserable. Noah was so unwell. He was on a ventilator several times. His first surgery wasn't done correctly and had to be redone. I can remember watching Noah pull chunks of his own hair out of his head because he was in such excruciating pain. I insisted to the surgeon that something was wrong, but the surgeon and hospital staff kept telling me that Noah was just suffering from gas pain. I could see that Noah's pain was continuing and that it was far more extreme than gas pain. The horror that I saw in his eyes is something that I can still remember today. I begged the doctors to do something. Finally they took him back into the OR and were shocked when they found that his intense pain was caused by gangrene. As a result, the doctors had to remove a part of his intestines. I watched him suffer all the time, and it hurt me so much. I wondered why God would allow so much suffering for such a little boy. On the outside I probably looked fine and like I was managing things well. Inside, I was so unhappy and unfilled. In times like these we search and search. We try to fill the empty places, and we even expect that our loved ones would fill those spaces for us. We feel dissatisfied when they can't fill them. We might wonder if God hears our prayers and if he even cares. *"I have been anxiously searching for you."*

A short time after Noah's passing, we were so relieved to get a call from a doctor who had an answer for us! Finally—after all those years of praying and searching, we were told that Braden had a duplication on his X chromosome. This duplication caused a syndrome called MECP2 duplication syndrome. Noah's frozen blood also confirmed that MECP2 duplication syndrome was what he had suffered from.

I wonder sometimes if God in his perfect timing waited until after Braden was born to reveal the boys' diagnosis to us. If we had known the diagnosis earlier and were informed that Noah had a genetic syndrome, we never would have thought about having another child. Braden wouldn't have existed. God wanted us to have a second son. God wanted Braden to be born. When I look back, I can see that God has used each of my boys to proclaim Jesus. In their quiet way, my boys' lives have touched the lives of so many. "Before I formed you in the womb I knew you, before you were born I set you apart" (Jeremiah 1:5).

Sometimes I feel like Braden is fighting every day to survive. He fights debilitating congestion on a daily basis. He has many exhausting seizures each day. These seizures wreak havoc on his body and cause regression. I have watched these seizures take away his ability to eat by mouth. The seizures have robbed him of his ability to hold his head up. The seizures are relentless and vicious. Some nights I have to give him inhalers and nebulizer treatments and do deep suctioning over and over all night. Many nights I fall into bed and I'm exhausted. I feel helpless watching him struggle to breathe. As seizures violently shake his little body, I beg God to make them stop. On nights like these (and there are many), I pray for God to hold me and give me strength to keep going. He is there. And he does. He gives me the strength that I don't have without him. My house isn't filled with the kind of peace that I used to imagine and long for. It is filled with the sounds of beeping monitors and suction machines, but my heart is filled with God's peace.

I remember being asked one time what I will do when my son is too big for me to carry. The question made me angry. I thought, "What will I do?! He can't sit unassisted, crawl, stand, or walk. Why would someone ask me that?" At that time of my journey I didn't know what to say. Truly, I didn't know what I would do and it scared me. Now, at this point in my journey with God, I would reply to that question with this answer: TRUST GOD. I WILL TRUST GOD. I know that he will be with me no matter what our family faces. My heart has peace about this when my eyes are focused on my God.

At this point in my life, I feel closer to God than I ever did before. I know where that peace that I was searching for can be found. That peace isn't found because a family's home doesn't have beeping machines. It isn't found in chasing and passing the ball with your children. It is found in Christ and the hope of an eternity in heaven with him. I get such peace from the knowledge that my boys will be completely healed one day. It didn't happen on earth with Noah, and it may not with Braden either. I know, though, with absolute certainty that in heaven my boys will be completely healed. This earthly life is only temporary. I don't need to anxiously search for God. I know that he is truly present.

❤ ❤ ❤

**I know where that peace
that I was searching
for can be found.**

Every day I miss my son Noah. This is an intense pain that will always be a part of my earthly life. Through all of this with both of my boys, God has been working inside of me. Through the Holy Spirit and God's Word, I am able to keep my eyes on my Savior. I'm not searching frantically for earthly satisfactions. God fills all of my empty spaces. God has changed me because of my boys. My boys have been mostly nonverbal, but God has used their sweet personalities and precious lives to change so many others.

My focus on my Savior has become clearer. Because of this, our marriage is also stronger. Our daughter loves the Lord and exudes his love. Family members and friends have been changed by knowing my boys. We have had the opportunity to share Christ's love with so many others because of the boys. Each of my children is a blessing, and God has used each of their young lives in mighty ways. He continues to use them for his glory each day. When I read Jeremiah 29:11, I know that God has plans and a purpose for our family, and I thank him for carrying us through this journey and letting us see glimpses of his great purpose. There is no wondering. God is truly present.

Pam Albert and her husband, Scot, are the parents of three children. Their two sons were born with MECP2 duplication syndrome.

CHAPTER 8

$$\heartsuit\ \heartsuit\ \heartsuit$$

Struggling
to Understand

MARGO'S STORY

"His mother said to him, 'Son, why have you treated us like this? Your father and I have been anxiously searching for you.' 'Why were you searching for me?' he asked. 'Didn't you know I had to be in my Father's house?' But they did not understand what he was saying to them. Then he went down to Nazareth with them and was obedient to them. But his mother treasured all these things in her heart. And Jesus grew in wisdom and stature, and in favor with God and man" (Luke 2:48-52).

Certainly in this situation Mary didn't see the big picture of her son as the world's Savior. She seems to have been focused on him only as her 12-year-old who was "lost." Even after she found Jesus in his Father's house and he explained his purpose there, the Bible tells us, "But they did not understand what he was saying to them."

"But they did not understand what he was saying to them." This was often true of the disciples as well. Many times it is recorded

that Jesus said things and it is clear from their reactions that the disciples didn't understand the bigger picture. There were many situations where he told them to do things or he did things or he said things, and the disciples really didn't understand the complete picture of what was going on.

This happens to us more often than we realize. It happens with other people. They tell us something, but we don't understand. We might think that we understand. Often when there has been a misunderstanding, time clears things up. As events unfold, true understanding dawns on us. "THIS is what they meant!"

Our understanding of God's Word and the way we apply it to our lives can be that way too. We read God's Word and we think we understand its meaning in our life. We look at our life circumstances and we try to see the bigger, eternal picture. As life goes on, we realize that what God was showing us or telling us was different than what we were looking for. God's Word is certainly unchanging, but our understanding changes as we mature and our circumstances change.

Sometimes when hard things happen and we search for God's plan and purpose within those hard things, we just don't understand why God does the things he does or what he is doing in or with our lives. It is such a blessing that we know he is an amazing God and worthy of our total trust—even in the face of difficulty. It is so soothing to our human hearts when he allows us to see glimpses of his eternal plan within our circumstances.

❤ MARGO'S STORY ❤

Sonja was born late on a Wednesday night and came home with us on Friday. We were brand-new parents, so we didn't really know how babies and feeding and parenting were supposed to go, but our gut feeling was that something didn't seem right with Sonja's feeding. We even noticed that she turned a little bit blue during one feeding attempt.

Sonja (at not quite four days old) and I stayed home from church that first Sunday morning. I had shared with my friend Pat, who was also a neonatal nurse, my concerns with Sonja. She was especially concerned with my description of Sonja turning blue, so she came to take baby Sonja and me to the clinic. My husband, Steve, had been at church that morning, but we knew the church service had just ended, so we stopped to let him know where we were headed. He hopped in and came along.

The doctor at the clinic didn't know what to make of the situation and was about to send us home when Sonja suddenly stopped breathing. This apnea episode lasted for about 10 seconds. The doctor's demeanor suddenly changed. He quickly took Sonja's vital signs. Sonja's temperature was only 92 degrees. *"But they did not understand what he was saying to them."*

At that moment I didn't understand the bigger picture, but I realized the graveness of the situation. I stated simply, "We're baptizing her now." Steve performed the baptism there at the clinic—Pat became Sonja's godmother. Sonja was going to be admitted to the hospital. She spent four days at the local hospital in Jacksonville, North Carolina, having every imaginable test run on her to no avail.

I rarely left Sonja's side. I monitored every episode of apnea and measured every cubic centimeter of nutrition that she took in. After four days the doctor admitted that he was stumped and announced that Sonja would be transferred to Duke University Hospital. Though we were living off of several days of almost no sleep, there was no question of whether or not to go along in our minds. We got into our car to follow the ambulance up to Durham, a two-and-a-half hour drive.

At Duke I had to endure the frustration of seeing all the tests that had been performed on my tiny eight-day-old daughter repeated. Duke hospital was not going to simply rely on the results of the tests performed at the "podunk" hospital in Jacksonville, so they redid everything and then did some other tests as well.

It was an incredible strain on me to watch as Sonja had blood drawn and spinal fluid tapped and to still have no answers. I can remember thinking that Sonja was just too tiny to be having all of this done to her. It was as if I could feel her pain. *"But they did not understand what he was saying to them."*

For two weeks in our little hospital room, Steve and I were able to bond with our sweet baby—and pray. A CD of children's Bible songs played almost nonstop. We knew that little Sonja belonged to God, having been adopted by God through Baptism into his family. Yet it was a struggle for me to "release" my baby into the care of hospital staff and even to the care of God. *"But they did not understand what he was saying to them."*

I was so eager for my baby to be well. I wanted to get her home where we could get decent sleep and food and regain our energy. Everything was waiting for little Sonja there: a lavender painted room and white baby furniture. The diapers and wipes were stocked. The closet held many darling little outfits just waiting to be worn.

———— ❤ ❤ ❤ ————

I felt that if I prayed often enough and trusted the Lord firmly enough, Sonja could receive the miracle of complete healing.

Finally, after three weeks of hospitals, we were given a diagnosis—Sonja had experienced a lack of oxygen sometime around birth. The subsequent brain damage would eventually be termed a form of cerebral palsy. This would prevent Sonja from speaking intelligibly, walking on her own, or even feeding herself. Sonja was sent home with an apnea monitor. We went home with our precious baby, but also with heads and hearts full of thoughts, questions, and prayers. *"But they did not understand what he was saying to them."*

We continued to measure and record Sonja's nutrition intake for the first year of her life. The daily care that she required took most of my waking time. God was graceful even in that circumstance, as Sonja was our first child so we didn't know any other reality with raising a child.

Early in our journey, I felt that if I prayed often enough and trusted the Lord firmly enough, Sonja could receive the miracle of complete healing and life could go on in a "normal" way. *"But they did not understand what he was saying to them."* As time went on, I realized that while God certainly had the power to fully heal Sonja, I really needed Sonja to be exactly who God made her to be. I needed the lesson of living in the joy of salvation.

One of Sonja's favorite DVD series is *Signing Time*. Rachel Coleman teaches signs in the most creative and interesting way. She adds songs to practice these signs. One song includes these words: "Maybe we won't find easy, but baby we found the good." Sonja perseveres, personifies patience, and, even though she cannot speak, is so honest with her feelings that I am not acquainted with a more genuine person.

It's all about the basics with Sonja: good food, a soft pillow, fun entertainment, and Jesus. The other day I asked her what she wanted to do, and she went to her hymns on her communicator. I said, "Sonja, if you want to have Bible time say 'yes,'" and without hesitation she nodded her head. One of her favorite Bible verses is "Whoever follows me will never walk in darkness, but will have the light of life" (John 8:12). You can see that light in Sonja's eyes, and when she smiles she simply radiates joy.

When she was 14 and a half, Sonja had her first seizure. It was scary for me, but I kept repeating the name above all others: "Jesus." He got us through that minute and two other episodes of the same duration in subsequent months. This experience helped me to respect Sonja at a greater level, adult to a younger adult. I feel a deeper sense of admiration for the graceful way she handles the challenges that comprise her cross. I admit that I questioned the Lord: "Isn't the fact that she can't balance, speak our words, or walk enough?" Oh, me of little faith. Just like Mary and the disciples, we don't always understand or see the big picture of why God allows the things that he does. One heavenly day I will know all the reasons why, and that just might coincide with the first time Sonja speaks—addressing her praises to the one who took care of the greatest of her special needs, the need that we each have, that of a Savior.

Nearly 15 years later, caring for Sonja can still be taxing, but she continues to be an amazing source of joy. Every goal she achieves is a cause for celebration and thanksgiving. She is alive. And, most important, she is alive in Jesus.

Margo and Steve Schmidt are the parents of two daughters. Their oldest, Sonja, has cerebral palsy.

CHAPTER 9

Why Do You Involve Me?

"JENNIFER'S" STORY

"On the third day a wedding took place at Cana in Galilee. Jesus' mother was there, and Jesus and his disciples had also been invited to the wedding. When the wine was gone, Jesus' mother said to him, 'They have no more wine.' 'Woman, why do you involve me?' Jesus replied. 'My hour has not yet come.' His mother said to the servants, 'Do whatever he tells you.' Nearby stood six stone water jars, the kind used by the Jews for ceremonial washing, each holding from twenty to thirty gallons. Jesus said to the servants, 'Fill the jars with water'; so they filled them to the brim. Then he told them, 'Now draw some out and take it to the master of the banquet.' They did so, and the master of the banquet tasted the water that had been turned into wine. He did not realize where it had come from, though the servants who had drawn the water knew. Then he called the bridegroom aside and said, 'Everyone brings out the choice wine first and then the cheaper wine after the guests have had too much to drink; but you have saved the best till now.' What Jesus did here in Cana of Galilee was the first of the signs through which he revealed his glory; and his disciples believed in him" (John 2:1-11).

"'Woman, why do you involve me?' Jesus replied. 'My hour has not yet come.' His mother said to the servants, 'Do whatever he tells you.'" Sometimes when I pray, I wonder if Jesus is saying to me, "Woman, why do you involve me?" I wonder if he has cast my prayers off and forgotten me. In this story, Mary doesn't seem deterred at all by Jesus' words to her. She wholly trusts him and says to the servants, "Do whatever he tells you." She has utter confidence that he not only can help her, but that he will. And Jesus does.

❤ "JENNIFER'S" STORY ❤

A few days before my daughter's 17th birthday, she came home from school and told me that she was suspended from school. I tried to get her to tell me why, but she just wouldn't share.

My husband and I were the type of parents who were present at our daughter's school whenever we could be. We attended "Carrie's" parent-teacher conferences, open houses, and special events. We chaperoned her field trips. We participated in parent advisory meetings and attended school board meetings. We were there. We saw Carrie's staff regularly, and they were familiar with us. Carrie has a cognitive disability, so getting the full story from her could be tricky. Because she couldn't or wouldn't share the information about her suspension with us, we were eager to hear from the school staff about what had happened.

The assistant principal from the high school called me. He told me that a male student with a learning disability had inappropriately touched Carrie. During our phone call, the assistant principal didn't give me many details. He told me that the incident was "taken care of" and that if I had any further questions or wanted to discuss it, I could call the SRO (school resource officer). He told me that because of this incident, my daughter was being suspended and could return to school in three days.

I hung up the phone feeling extremely upset and confused. What had happened to Carrie? How had the situation been "taken care of"? Could I safely send her back to school at the end of the three days? Why was my vulnerable daughter being punished with a suspension for being victimized? Would Carrie even be willing to go back to a school where she might no longer feel safe? Was the school's staff truly concerned enough about Carrie's safety and well-being? When we cry out to God in times like this, times when our vulnerable children are hurt and unprotected, does God answer, *"Woman, why do you involve me?"*

The next day I was able to talk to the SRO. I was given more details about the situation. The male student had taken Carrie by the arm and led her into the restroom. He had locked the bathroom door and then had her undress above the waist so that he could see and touch her. The two of them were locked in the restroom for only a brief time, approximately three minutes, before the end of the class period. Only three minutes, but three minutes in which my vulnerable daughter was not protected by the school staff who were supposed to be protecting her. Those three minutes may have harmed her extensively. Every day I entrusted my daughter's protection not only to the school staff but also to my Lord in prayer. Was this how he answered my prayer: "*Woman, why do you involve me?*"

In that meeting with the SRO we learned that the boy had also tried to inappropriately touch two other girls. These girls reported the incident to staff members. They questioned the boy, and he actually confessed his behavior toward Carrie too. The SRO explained that since my daughter had not said no, the school considered her to be partially at fault for the incident. The other two girls were dealt with differently because they had clearly told the boy no. Every day I entrusted my daughter's protection not only to the school staff but also to my Lord in prayer. Was this how he answered my prayer: "*Woman, why do you involve me?*"

The SRO went on to tell me that the boy had a very thick file that included similar behavioral trouble in the past. For this particular incident, he was suspended from school for three days—the same as his victim, my Carrie. He also would have some his classes switched so that he was no longer in any classes with the girls he had victimized.

I was raised to respect authority, but I also thought that those in authority protected the vulnerable. I left this meeting in a total state of confusion. It felt to me like the

SRO, a police officer meant to keep the students at the high school safe, was just sweeping this under the rug. Not only were they sweeping this under the rug, but they seemed to be calling my daughter guilty by punishing her. How could they punish a victim? Every day I entrusted my daughter's protection not only to the school staff but also to my Lord in prayer. Was this how he answered my prayer: *"Woman, why do you involve me?"*

— ❤ ❤ ❤ —

Not only were they sweeping this under the rug, but they seemed to be calling my daughter guilty by punishing her.

I decided that I needed to make the best of things for Carrie. I enjoyed some extra time at home with her during her suspension. I nurtured and reassured her. Then I sent her back to school with the assurance from the school staff that she would not cross paths with this boy anymore. My confidence in her safety at school and in the staff was certainly shaken. As I continued to investigate the incident, it became obvious that it had been improperly handled. It was never truly resolved to my satisfaction, but my daughter was safe and that was the important thing.

I am so thankful that God gave me a mother's intuition and the confidence to listen to it. My daughter was a victim of sexual assault and, whether the school wanted to sweep it under the rug or not, she needed me to be her protector and defender. When I prayed, God did not cast my prayers away. He listened. It may have seemed at first as if he wasn't listening. He allowed that boy to hurt my Carrie. He allowed the school staff to place blame on her. When I asked him for protection for my family, was he saying, *"Woman, why do you involve me?"* He wasn't. God didn't abandon Carrie or me.

When I look back on this truly terrible incident, although it was never resolved in a very satisfying way, I can truly see that God was with us in all of the small ways that support came. He was right there and covering us in his protection and love. God gave me friends who were able to point me to the right people for help and guidance. He directed us to a police officer who would guide us to a better understanding of the situation and how the SRO should have handled it. God had protected Carrie in the situation by limiting the time that this boy had to victimize her. The boy had only three minutes because the bell rang for classes to change. Yes, the situation was completely mishandled, and I continue to pray that the school leaders will see their errors and go about things better in the future. Yet God was there even in this mishandled situation. Carrie was kept from further harm. I praise God for his protection. As time has passed, his presence and healing have become so evident to me. Even when such terrible things happen, I can be still in the knowledge of God who never mishandles any situation. He carries us through these difficult things and can use even the worst treatment to bring glory to his name.

God is our refuge and strength,
an ever-present help in trouble.
Therefore we will not fear,
though the earth give way
and the mountains fall into the heart of the sea,
though its waters roar and foam
and the mountains quake with their surging.
There is a river whose streams
make glad the city of God,
the holy place where the Most High dwells.
God is within her, she will not fall;
God will help her at break of day.
Nations are in uproar, kingdoms fall;
he lifts his voice, the earth melts.

The LORD Almighty is with us;
the God of Jacob is our fortress.

Come and see what the LORD has done,
the desolations he has brought on the earth.
He makes wars cease to the ends of the earth.
He breaks the bow and shatters the spear;
he burns the shields with fire.
He says, "Be still, and know that I am God;
I will be exalted among the nations,
I will be exalted in the earth."

The LORD Almighty is with us;
the God of Jacob is our fortress. (Psalm 46)

This mother and family have chosen to remain anonymous, so the names have been changed. All other information is factual.

CHAPTER 10

Blessed Among Women?
WENDY'S STORY
(CONTINUED)

"Near the cross of Jesus stood his mother, his mother's sister, Mary the wife of Clopas, and Mary Magdalene. When Jesus saw his mother there, and the disciple whom he loved standing nearby, he said to her, 'Woman, here is your son,' and to the disciple, 'Here is your mother.' From that time on, this disciple took her into his home" (John 19:25-27).

Imagine it. Your son. Choosing to live on the edges of society. Living a strange sort of life. Different from the norm. Itinerant. Homeless. Sharing a message that few want to hear. Hated. Unfairly accused. Beaten. Whipped. Mocked. And then finally, crucified. A crown of thorns pressed into his head. Hands and feet pierced with nails. Can you imagine watching his life unfold? Later, can you imagine standing on Golgotha at the foot of his cross? Can you imagine standing beside this man whom you have loved for his entire life—since before his first breath—as he is brutally killed? Imagine that this man is the son who was born from your body. He is your son whom you held, loved, and nourished with your own milk. He is the son whose knees you cleaned and tears you dried as a small boy. He is the son whom you have loved with the ferocious and consuming love of a mother. It is so difficult to think about the suffering and death of Jesus when we think of our Savior. How much more intimate was the pain of Jesus' death for Mary? When Simeon told Mary, "And a sword will pierce your own soul too" (Luke 2:35), it was a prediction of this very moment. Jesus was Mary's Savior, but he was also her son.

A little over three decades before this, Mary sang a beautiful song of praise to the God who had just chosen her to be the mother of his Son. I wonder if as she stood at the foot of that dear son's cross she thought of her words of praise.

> "My soul glorifies the Lord
> and my spirit rejoices in God my Savior,
> for he has been mindful
> of the humble state of his servant.
> From now on all generations
> will call me blessed,
> for the Mighty One has done
> great things for me—
> holy is his name." (Luke 1:46-49)

I wonder if Mary felt blessed among women as her son breathed his last breath. I wonder if her first instinct was to sing to God for doing great things for her and through her. Yet we know that God truly was doing *great* deeds through Mary. Right there, through Mary's suffering son, the greatest deed in the history of the world was being done. Mary's heart was torn in two like the curtain of the temple that day. This happened so that the world could have eternal hope, but I imagine that in that moment Mary couldn't think about the purpose, but only of her dear son's pain. My chest physically aches when I think of Mary at the foot of that cross. Oh, how she must have hurt! Yet God had an eternal plan for Mary's good and the good of the whole world.

I can remember holding my own small son. He would have been about 14 months old. He couldn't sit up. He wasn't trying to say any words. He could hardly hold a toy to play with. Our daytime life was filled with therapies and doctors, and our nights with waking and nursing. (My son nursed every 2-3 hours around the clock for 32 months. It was exhausting!) We had been visiting specialists for months trying to discover why our Liam wasn't developing as babies should. As Liam's older sister napped and I dozed and held him one afternoon, the phone rang. Our pediatrician was on the other end of the line. He rattled off a bunch of terms that I didn't really understand. He said that Liam's genetic tests had shown something! I was happy! Yes! I thought, "Now we can fix what is wrong." As the next few days went by and we got more information about Liam's condition, I realized that there is nothing to celebrate when it comes to MECP2 duplication syndrome. There would be no fixing. The prognosis was grim. My heart was broken.

My heart ached for Liam, who would never live a normal life. It ached for his sister, who would never enjoy a typical sibling relationship. It ached for me because so many of my dreams and hopes and plans went up in smoke that afternoon. My world truly shifted on its axis that afternoon.

In the same moments that I begged God to take Liam, I loved him fiercely.

As the next year went by, I spent hours and hours crying. I was hurting and angry. I knew little about disability, but I knew that I wanted nothing to do with it. I even begged God to take Liam to be with him. I wanted a different son, a whole one. I wanted a son without a disability. In the same moments that I begged God to take Liam, I loved him fiercely. I wanted him and I wanted to do everything that I could to help him. Those feelings are the true dichotomy of the days right after diagnosis.

A few short months after that, I begged God not to take my son to be with him. I stood next to a small hospital bed as Liam gasped for air. I begged God to clear his little lungs. I learned to deep suction my own son (awful to do, but works wonders!). I learned to use home oxygen and to give nebulizers. I learned to do chest therapy. I got my "RN" in Liam-care.

A year after that, I praised God as my son learned to crawl. A few years later, I watched him "walk" upright in a gait trainer to accept a certificate for finishing his early childhood program. Very recently, I celebrated Liam's excellent use of an augmentative communication device and watched him use it to "say" his line in his school's first grade program—right along with his typical peers.

I have daily thanked God for the slobbery kisses and sweet smiles that Liam gives. I have held my son through nights and days of illness. I have advocated for his school services and medical needs. I have read the same books hundreds of times and played the same games and puzzles in the repetitive ways that only children with autistic tendencies can appreciate. I have read these same exact books and played these same exact games not for days, not for months, but for years. I have rejoiced when Liam meets milestones. Our special-needs life has been so rewarding and exhausting and emotional and blessed and wonderful, but it has never been easy.

Although we have some periods of respite, I am quite certain that our life with Liam will get harder as time goes on, not easier. Liam gets bigger every day and still has not learned to stand or walk without support. It is getting almost impossible for me to lift him without help. This makes diaper changes, toileting, baths, putting him to bed, taking him places, and feeding him very difficult. As Liam's understanding of communication grows, he is more demanding and less patient with delays. The need for us to find the right people and technology for him to communicate is ever on my mind. His sensory sensitivities make activities outside of our home very difficult. While some of his sensitivities seem to get better with age, others seem to become worse. Liam's syndrome also causes seizures in almost every individual who has it. With these seizures come aspirations, pneumonia, severe regression of functional skills, fatigue, and many other side effects. I pray that God will allow Liam to remain seizure free.

It would be so easy to look at our life and feel abandoned by God. I could wonder where he is in all of this. My hurt is so big. It eats at my chest and consumes me at times. I could look on my son whose life isn't what I expected and wonder why my God allows this because the ache in my heart throbs so intensely at times. I could stand next to this boy who I have nursed and loved and whose tears I have dried and despise the God who chose me to be his mother because I am so very broken by his differences. But this is the thing: MECP2 duplication syndrome does not change who my God is. Liam's circumstances do not change who God is. When Liam meets milestones and we celebrate, God is good. When Liam starts seizures someday, God will still be the same good God.

The same God who parted the seas and tumbled the walls of Jericho and enabled a little boy's stone to kill a giant— HE is in our special needs lives. He uses me. He uses Liam. He uses Liam's sisters. He uses you. He uses your children. He has purpose and a plan for us—a beautiful, eternal purpose and plan.

This God loves you. He loved you enough that he gave HIS ONLY son. It wasn't only Mary whose heart ached as she watched her son suffer on Golgatha. God's heart ached too. "He gave his one and only Son" . . . for you. And me. And my children. And yours. Why? "That whoever believes in him shall not perish but have eternal life" (John 3:16)— so that we can live in eternity with him forever. He did it for us. He didn't have to. He chose to—the truest love there is.

God knows our pain. He cries with us. He knows our weakness, and he carries us.

> Be merciful to me, LORD, for I am in distress;
>   my eyes grow weak with sorrow,
>   my soul and body with grief.
> My life is consumed by anguish
>   and my years by groaning;
> my strength fails because of my affliction,
> and my bones grow weak. (Psalm 31:9,10)

God is the thread that runs through each of our stories. God's presence. God's provision. God's love. God's protection. Whether our life story is that of painful diagnosis and medical treatments or that of feeling left out of regular life. Whether we are early in our story with babies and toddlers or later with adult children or children who are already enjoying the presence of Jesus, God is with us and our children. God is for us. He took care of our deepest need on that hill of Calvary. He is in each moment of our earthly lives. May each of us feel his presence, provision, protection, and love daily.

There are still times when I need to be reminded of God's control and plan in my life. At these times, I often turn to

Isaiah chapter 40. Without getting into the history and politics of what Isaiah was writing about, his words here were meant for the Israelites in one of their darkest hours, when they were wondering if they were still God's special people. Conquered, not in control of their lives at all, wondering if God would ever work in their midst again and even if he *could* do so—in this chapter, God answers all of that by speaking his absolute comfort through the prophet Isaiah. These words are also meant to comfort us today. They remind us of God's provision and plan for our lives and assure us of his ultimate provision of a Savior for our sins. Whatever seems out of control and hopeless is within the power of God because he is Lord of creation. These verses soothe me and fill me with confidence in a God who is so big and whose love is so amazing. Reading them fills my being with peace.

> Comfort, comfort my people,
>   says your God.
> Speak tenderly to Jerusalem,
>   and proclaim to her
> that her hard service has been completed,
>   that her sin has been paid for,
> that she has received from the LORD's hand
>   double for all her sins.
>
> A voice of one calling:
> "In the wilderness prepare
>   the way for the LORD;
> make straight in the desert
>   a highway for our God.
> Every valley shall be raised up,

every mountain and hill made low;
the rough ground shall become level,
the rugged places a plain.
And the glory of the
LORD will be revealed,
and all people will see it together.
For the mouth of the
LORD has spoken."

A voice says, "Cry out."
And I said, "What shall I cry?"

"All people are like grass,
and all their faithfulness is like
the flowers of the field.
The grass withers and the flowers fall,
because the breath of the
LORD blows on them.
Surely the people are grass.
The grass withers and the flowers fall,
but the word of our God endures forever."

You who bring good news to Zion,
go up on a high mountain.
You who bring good news to Jerusalem,
lift up your voice with a shout,
lift it up, do not be afraid;
say to the towns of Judah,
"Here is your God!"

See, the Sovereign LORD comes with power,
and he rules with a mighty arm.
See, his reward is with him,

and his recompense accompanies him.
He tends his flock like a shepherd:
He gathers the lambs in his arms
and carries them close to his heart;
he gently leads those that have young.

Who has measured the waters
in the hollow of his hand,
or with the breadth of his hand
marked off the heavens?
Who has held the dust of the earth in a basket,
or weighed the mountains on the scales
and the hills in a balance?
Who can fathom the Spirit of the LORD,
or instruct the LORD as his counselor?

"To whom will you compare me?
Or who is my equal?" says the Holy One.
Lift up your eyes and look to the heavens:
Who created all these?
He who brings out the starry host one by one
and calls forth each of them by name.
Because of his great power and mighty strength,
not one of them is missing.

Why do you complain, Jacob?
Why do you say, Israel,
"My way is hidden from the LORD;
my cause is disregarded by my God"?
Do you not know?
Have you not heard?
The LORD is the everlasting God,
the Creator of the ends of the earth.

He will not grow tired or weary,
and his understanding no one can fathom.
He gives strength to the weary
and increases the power of the weak.
Even youths grow tired and weary,
and young men stumble and fall;
but those who hope in the LORD
will renew their strength.
They will soar on wings like eagles;
they will run and not grow weary,
they will walk and not be faint.
(Isaiah 40:1-13,25-31)

EPILOGUE

Today was the first time in several months that I have opened my copy of this book. As I read it again, a comment from one reader was on my mind: "It seemed that you and all of the other mothers who shared their stories in your book had a fairly mature faith before kids with disabilities entered the picture."

It is true that I have never *not* known Jesus. I have been taught about Jesus and that I am loved by my Savior for my entire life. Our family, friends, and church family rallied around us in such spectacular ways after Liam's diagnosis and in the years since. They have truly been the hands and feet of Christ in our life, and we feel his love through their support. Liam's diagnosis played out in ways that drew compassion from people. Liam is a joyful, sweet boy who brings out the best in every person that he meets. He is easy for others to love, and, perhaps, because of that we have always felt very supported. From the dozens of special-needs moms I have spoken with these last few years, I know that many families do not receive the kind of support that we have and I am truly saddened by that.

Faith and earthly supports make a huge difference in the way we perceive God's presence when life is difficult. They help us to keep sight of our eternal hope even in the midst of earthly hardships. Sometimes, when it seems the people in our lives have deserted us, we mistakenly understand that as evidence that God has deserted us too.

What kind of faith would I have if it weren't for all the support I have enjoyed? if people, especially those who should know better, were cruel toward Liam instead of loving? I don't know.

Maybe God would keep my faith going like he did for "Jennifer" in chapter 9. She did not have an overwhelmingly positive outcome to her story. If a reporter got hold of her story, it wouldn't be used as the "feel good" segment on the five o'clock news. The support and help that she got from the school were very much lacking, perhaps even criminal. Yet with an anger-free heart of faith that I can hardly understand, "Jennifer" can look back and see God's hand in subtle ways. Through the Holy Spirit, she can rest in God's grace. Peace in such a situation can only be from the Lord.

Or I think about "Jane" in chapter 5 and her intense hurt and rejection over not being welcome to bring her son to church anymore. Somehow she did not turn her back on church altogether over that. God kept her close to him.

Yes, I realize that several of the moms whose stories were told *did* start their journeys with a pretty mature faith or with fantastic church families or extensive support systems. I'm not sure if Mary had much support as she faced her unexpected life. But I do know that Mary and each of us mothers in this book were rocked to the core for days on end by the suffering and troubles of our children. I know that as humans, we each fight our sinful nature whenever we face difficult diagnoses and situations with our children. Our human hearts see only earthly purposes and goals, and we want to judge God by those standards. We aren't special, amazing, superhuman moms.

None of us eagerly submits our children to hardship or death so that the work of God can be done. We just don't. We are human moms and we desperately love our children. We would give our own comfort and lives to spare them.

But we have found that God is there for desperate, confused, heartbroken mothers. He'll be there for you too, even if no one else is.

I can remember shortly after Liam was diagnosed that I was watching our pastor's wife in church. They have five adult children, and their youngest is a young man in his twenties who has Down syndrome. I was watching her happily sitting by her son before church, and I angrily thought, "Well, she might be happy with God allowing this in her life, but I sure won't be!!!" I felt really angry at the plot twist in my life and felt ferociously dedicated to my own misery. In that moment I felt mad at the pastor's wife for being okay with God allowing special needs into her family's life. Maybe you feel like that as you read about each of these moms?

The secret to navigating this hard, unplanned, special-needs life is not to somehow turn yourself into a hero of faith. It isn't to pretend things are easy and stamp down your hurts and put on a happy face. These hurts are too real. They are hurts that don't have a good earthly answer. The outcomes are usually not a total cure and then back to the life you always planned for.

There isn't a secret. There is only God. He is it. His Word reveals him to us. "The LORD is the everlasting God, the

Creator of the ends of the earth. He will not grow tired or weary, and his understanding no one can fathom" (Isaiah 40:28). When we bask in God's Word and get to know his character, we can rest in him even in the hardest of circumstances. He is the God who sacrificed his own Son for us on Calvary's cross. God is the only way we can have peace.

That doesn't mean it won't be hard or painful, even unimaginably so. It doesn't mean you will always *feel* rest and peace. It just means that our God knows. He is with us. He hears even the most tear-filled, angry, messed-up prayers to him. He works through all of it with our eternal good always in mind.

It is only the Holy Spirit in our hearts that enables us, at least a lot of the time, to look at our lives and our children's lives through the lens of eternity. When we use our "faith eyes" to look at life, we see that eternity is so much longer than this tragic, sin-hurting earthly life. This faith allows even the weakest among us to see that God can work through the worst of pain. It helps us to get small glimpses of his bigger plan and purpose.

I encourage you to go back through the book, find some of the passages or thoughts that comforted you most, and pray to God about them. Pray that he will use those words to heal your heart and open up your "faith eyes" wider than ever. Jesus promises, "If you then, though you are evil, know how to give good gifts to your children, how much more will your Father in heaven give the Holy Spirit to those who ask him!" (Luke 11:13). As we read and hear

God's Word, the Holy Spirit works and strengthens our faith so that we can trust God, at least enough to keep telling him how upset we are.

Mary was just a regular mom whom God used despite her weaknesses, confusion, and pain. At the very end of Jesus' life as he was dying on the cross, he asked his beloved disciple to provide and care for her (John 19:25-27). It is so profound to me that as he was paying for Mary's (and our) sins, he was thinking of his grief-stricken mother and her earthly provision. This book was written to tell you that he does no less for you. He loves you and has a plan for your eternal good. He loves your child. He is with you even in this. Especially in this.

Want more support?

**A church that will welcome
you and your child?**

Someone with a listening ear?

———— ❤ ❤ ❤ ————

Jesus Cares Ministries (JCM) assists
congregations in reaching out to people with
intellectual and developmental disabilities,
their families, and their communities. To find
a JCM program near you, to learn more
about our resources, or just to be encouraged
in your important work as a mom, please
email us at jcm@tlha.org.